What is Beautiful in the Sky

Michael Harding is an author and playwright. His creative chronicle of ordinary Irish life is published as a weekly column in *The Irish Times*. He has written numerous plays for the Abbey Theatre, including Una Pooka, Misogynist and Sour Grapes, and has published three novels, *Priest*, *The Trouble with Sarah Gullion* and *Bird in the Snow* as well as the award-winning, bestselling memoir, *Staring at Lakes* (Winner of the Bord Gáis Energy Book of the Year), and *Hanging with the Elephant*, *Talking to Strangers*, *On Tuesdays I'm a Buddhist* and *Chest Pain*. He also has a regular podcast with reflections on life on Patreon.

MICHAEL
HARDING

What is
Beautiful
in the Sky

HACHETTE
BOOKS
IRELAND

First published in Ireland in 2020 by
HACHETTE BOOKS IRELAND

1

Cataloguing in Publication Data is available from the British Library

ISBN: 9781473691018

Book design and typesetting: Anú Design, Tara

Printed and bound by Clays Ltd, Elcograf S.p.A

Hachette Books Ireland policy is to use papers that are natural, renewable and recyclable products
and made from wood grown in sustainable forests. The logging and manufacturing processes are
expected to conform to the environmental regulations of the country of origin.

Hachette Books Ireland
8 Castlecourt Centre
Castleknock
Dublin 15, Ireland

A division of Hachette UK Ltd
Carmelite House, 50 Victoria Embankment, EC4Y 0DZ

www.hachettebooksireland.ie

Praise for Michael Harding

'Harding is a self-deprecating and winsome writer whose bittersweet musings on middle-age, loneliness and the search for spiritual enlightenment ... are leavened by an incredibly dry and unforced wit'
Metro Herald

'Often funny, occasionally disturbing and not without its moments of deep sadness, Harding has peeled back his soul and held it out on the palm of his hand for all to see'
Christine Dwyer-Hickey

'A repository of modern man's deepest fears, Harding emerges as something of an embattled hero for our times ... It's rare for a memoir to demand such intense emotional involvement, and rarer still for it to be so fully rewarded'
Sunday Times

'Hilarious, and tender, and mad, and harrowing, and wistful, and always beautifully written. A wonderful book'
Kevin Barry

'I read this book in one sitting ... Beautifully written ... *Staring at Lakes* gives us permission to be lost, sick, sad, creative, happy and compassionate – in short, to be human'
Mary McEvoy, *Irish Independent*

For Tom MacIntyre
and Celine, his heroic champion and collaborator

Some of the names and details within this book have been changed.

Contents

A note from the author

A life is not a straight line. And a memoir is not a historically accurate account of a life. Memoir allows the story to become a lens for other stuff. So there are some events that I keep returning to in various volumes of my memoir, and some stories I present from different angles and in varying contexts.

Memoir, in the end, is a creative act, a fiction at the deepest level, wherein the author can reshape biography in different forms, not as a chronological history but as a song of joy to the simple mystery of life. Remembering becomes both an act of love and of gratitude.

Today Is the Day

I was surprised this morning by the heat. We'd been expecting rain. The forecast is for an end to the sunshine. All through the lockdown my consistent companion in the garden has been the sun. It was so hot that even the water tank dried up – something which hasn't happened in twenty-five years.

But things changed a few days ago. The sky filled with grey clouds. Met Éireann promised rain in the west and that usually means us.

It was as if the blue sky and the bright sun had stayed with us out of solidarity during the lockdown. To keep us warm inside and help us cope.

So when the sun rose a few hours ago over Sliabh an Iarainn and danced in a blue and empty sky, and knocked on the big glass windows of the bedroom, I felt it was calling to me and I went out barefoot just after 6 a.m. to examine the grass.

It's tight enough as it is, but another cut today would crown it, would turn it into a lawn as smart as any golf links.

You can't be too careful with the lawn when you live in Leitrim; it's vital to cut the grass immediately whenever a blue sky is given; there's nothing worse than saying, 'I'll do it tomorrow,' and then waking up to find it's pouring cats and dogs.

So even this morning as I rose from sleep and moved lightly across the floor so as not to waken the beloved, and as I slipped out the patio door, I had a purpose.

And I love this moment; always, I love this recurring moment, when I am alone with only the woodland around me, the cliff and lake and mountain before me. I feel wrapped in a mother's blanket.

I'm not religious enough to get up and pray, but the lawn is my rosary and the trees are my beads. I finger one as I walk. I observe my feet on the lawn to see if there is any dampness or if it is sufficiently dry to cut.

This walking at first light becomes almost an ecstasy in June, when the day begins at 4.30 a.m. and the divide between humans and all other animal life is at its widest. There are three or four hours each morning now when the garden is as clean and natural as it might have been had humans never emerged into the light of day.

This is the time when the trees around me and the grass beneath my feet feel like a mother's touch. I am awakening in my belonging as the morning breeze kisses my old face.

Although if rain comes tomorrow the midges will return, and kiss me too, or eat my face. And I saw a greenfly on the back of my hand, negotiating his way through the hairs.

I avoid walking close to the long grasses – the Yorkshire grass that rolls like a faint purple ocean along the ditch.

And the buttercup is still about. And the flag irises in the pond are early this year. And a tiny yellow gem with four petals that I heard described in Donegal as the Greek cross has taken root near the apple tree.

Everywhere on these mornings there are bees. Brown bees, bumblebees and little black bees. They've been feasting for weeks on the dandelion but now the Albertine roses are opening for them. The foxgloves have grown their steeples, and their purple flutes are wide-open caverns for the bees' delight and about twenty of them stand together in the shade of the woodland.

It would be blasphemous to fire up the lawnmower yet – the big four-stroke Honda that sits in the green shed, waiting for me. I go down and unlock the shed and ensure that my garden gloves are sitting on the handlebar of the lawnmower where I left them, that there is petrol in the tank and sufficient petrol in the red five-gallon container because I usually need about two fillings of petrol to finish the entire job. But I don't pull the starting cord because it is too early.

Instead I just walk about, noting how the yellow gorse has just about gone over, its flowers fading, but how the broom, almost the same plant to my eye, is bursting with yellow so densely luminous that a painter might reach out to it like a lover.

I get lyrical in these mornings. I cannot resist the glory of heaven in this ordinary place. And I am here. I am present. And today is the day we had been waiting for.

The Heat of the Sun

The lockdown arrived in Ireland at the end of March. But I knew it was

coming. I was alert to its imminent arrival four weeks earlier. Even when RTÉ asked me to travel for a radio interview in Dublin with Brendan O'Connor in late March, I said no. "I'm not moving," I told the researcher. She was a bit surprised. They had other guests travelling into the studio that morning.

'Well,' says I, 'they won't be coming into the studio this time next week.'

And I was right.

I had left Dublin on the sixth of March, after attending an event in City Hall the previous night to celebrate the work of the Samaritans in Ireland. It turned out to be the final time, although it was a week later, on the twelfth of March, that I realised clearly what was coming, and began to shutter myself away for hours each day in my study, alone in a self-imposed isolation. And when the lockdown officially arrived

I was well settled in the hills above Lough Allen with my beloved.

In the course of the following three months all that we were was taken. As a nation we became passive robots overnight and in particular the elderly cocooners – a word that lives phonetically between buffoon and baboon. People were masked and isolated in the shopping malls and garden centres, the supermarkets and the pharmacies, at a two-metre distance, even from loved ones when they fell ill. Some waved through glass windows at their relatives, even as they were dying. Some waved from car parks and waiting rooms and smoking areas through screens on their iPads to bid farewell.

Today, the seventh of June, I am finalising the manuscript I have written in that confinement. I worked every day in my studio at the back of the house and walked in the garden for exercise day and night for twelve weeks.

The garden is really a wilderness and comprises just under an acre of woodland, beside which is a small house, an artist's workshop, and my own shed or studio.

To the south is the woodland of between seventy and one hundred young trees. Holly, chestnut, Spanish chestnut, birch, guelder rose, beech, willow, Norwegian maple, oak, Canadian maple, Chilean beech. There is a carpet of bluebell, garlic and other wild flowers. The foxgloves grow in the shade, and have not yet reached their full height, nor have they yet come into bloom. That will happen in July.

To the north is the house, where the beloved still sleeps as I slip out the patio door and venture into the woodland. I walk through this grove of beech and birch and emerge to the east, looking further east, across the full length of Lough Allen and at Sliabh an Iarainn on the far shore.

At the perimeter is a wire fence with cement posts, protecting us from a cliff, a sixty-foot drop lined with gorse, where I walk until I come to my studio, in the north-east of the territory: a standalone building twenty-five feet by twenty-five feet with one patio door on the eastern side, offering me another view of the lake. There are two windows in the apex roof and a medium-sized window looking south to the woodland. I slide the door of my studio open and go inside.

It has been a long journey since January. I was in Warsaw and there was news of a virus in Wuhan, and it had not occurred to me what might be ahead. We were looking at a house for sale in Donegal and dreaming of being there by the first of May. I imagined a perfect sunny day, opening the door to begin a new life beside the sea. But when the first of May came along we were still in Leitrim, locked down, and the world had changed.

'O Mary, we crown thee with blossoms today,' as the children used to sing. But they didn't sing it in 2020.

We were taken away from a universe that was revolving around us, as if just for us, and we found ourselves back in a contingent strange and dangerous place, where we needed each other because we were vulnerable, and where it was us that spun around some centre in the cosmos we didn't quite comprehend.

The apex roof inside my studio creates a triangle with three pine crossbeams to buttress the walls and the space has a feeling of height more akin to a small church than to a workroom. Here began my complete silence.

I have two desks. A Georgian bureau from the late eighteenth century and a partners desk from the late nineteenth century, the work of the famous Maple Company of London, Paris and Buenos Aires. I bought these precious antiques from a dealer in Donegal. They are both aligned beneath the south-facing window and establish for me the very crucible of my work, as an altar might be the highest energy point of a well-built church. The big partners desk is the place where I sit every day to write my stories because I take my craft seriously. And of course I mean what I say in all my stories.

But the real magic of stories is that they don't contain the truth. They point to the truth. They are not the moon. They are the old person's finger in the boat standing up in the night and pointing to what is beautiful in the sky. And the young man or woman follows the finger, and sees the moon, and their heart opens to the moment.

That's what stories do. Or at least that is what they did in the long-ago time when people believed in stories. Not in the truth of them, but in the telling of them. The saying of them and the heart opening as it does in the listening.

And here now I sit again at my desk for one more day; to read over this story. To correct a few spellings. Integrate a few loose paragraphs. Question some of the details. Alter an occasional sentence. And most importantly to write an ending. It's always a moment of achievement for an author – to view the final draft one last time before another story is born.

I suppose if I never wrote another word, the person I would really miss writing about would be the General.

It's a long time ago that I first drowned the shamrock with him, in a Mullingar hotel in 2006 after I first arrived in Westmeath. It had been a time of great expectations; I was newly arrived in Mullingar and had begun writing a column in *The Irish Times* about ordinary life in the town. I felt I might be on the verge of great achievements. I mentioned to the General that I even intended climbing the Reek that year.

'Be careful about that,' he said.

I said, 'I shall wear climbing boots, so I don't sprain an ankle.'

He said, 'It's not the ankles you need to worry about, it's the wind.'

I said, 'You can't avoid wind if you're on a mountain.'

He said, 'You're not getting my point; mountain-climbing

is a useless and unnecessary exercise. And excessive exercise is widely recognised as a cause of flatulence.'

He should know; he breaks wind like an officer's horse, and usually excuses it by saying, 'I am becoming more like Doctor Swift by the day.'

As if his wind was as bracing a comment on modern society as one of Jonathan Swift's pamphlets might have been about the world he lived in.

'When a man exercises, he shakes up the innards, and the intestines are left like a leaking balloon; so beware of the mountain.'

We were sitting in the foyer. Green shamrocks had been painted on the windows. The receptionist wore a leprechaun hat, and the foyer was full of children in green uniforms.

The General finished his sixth pint of Guinness and belched pleasantly. 'And avoid cabbage,' he declared, 'at all costs. Bacon and cabbage are consumed by the Irish in unnatural quantities, but people don't realise that cabbage can do to the stomach what a lighted match does to a tank of petrol. I used to feed it to the horses years ago when I lived in Hampshire, the night before a hunt, to make them jump higher.'

'You may be correct about the cabbage,' I conceded, 'but nobody could accept that climbing a mountain is a cause of flatulence.'

'My good man,' he said, 'when I was meditating in India I always did yoga stretches before sitting; then when I began the meditation I often experienced methane bursting from various orifices. My guru explained that this initial period in the meditation session is known as 'the settling of the winds'. But I was only doing yoga; consider what you would be like after climbing the Reek.'

The General's massive eyebrows lifted, and he stared at me with great intensity.

Then looking towards the bar he bellowed, 'Bartender, two more pints of your finest stout, please.'

There was a tall woman sitting on a nearby sofa wrapped in a fur coat, and sipping from a long glass of something green, through a straw. She was listening to the General with great attention.

'Those hippie families in the west,' the General said, 'give their children nothing but lentils, and when the poor creatures go to school everybody laughs at them.'

The woman on the sofa rose. Clearly she had heard enough. She approached us and I dreaded what she might say.

'I kept chickens,' the General continued, 'when I lived in Kilkenny. I would cook one occasionally in a pot and make a hot curry, and by jingo if there was curry left over I fed it back to the other ones in the yard, and they lapped it up.'

I said, 'That's disgusting.'

'Ah yes,' he said, 'but they laid wonderfully spicy eggs.'

'Forgive me for interrupting,' the lady said, her eyes on the General, 'but I believe we knew each other when you lived in Kilkenny.'

The General's face brightened. 'Delia!' he exclaimed, with great excitement, and he stood to embrace her. And just then, and without the slightest embarrassment, he broke enough wind to sail an Armada.

'Oh don't mind me; it's only the Guinness,' he declared, as two more pints arrived on a tray, with little shamrocks imprinted on their creamy heads.

It was hardly 6 a.m. but my phone actually rang at this point in my re-reading of the script. And I smiled to see it was the General. When I answered, I heard him breathing with difficulty. For a moment I wondered had he caught the disease.

'You're up early,' I said. 'Are you OK?'

'Just tired,' he said. 'That's all. I can't sleep. And I'm fucking fed up with this. We have to get out tomorrow. We must meet. What say you to a lunch in Mullingar?'

I smiled. 'We can't,' I said. 'Tomorrow there are things opening but not everywhere. And there is no travel allowed yet outside your region. So no matter what opens tomorrow you are still stuck in Mullingar and I'm stuck in Leitrim.'

'Fuck that,' he whispered. 'Fuck that. I thought it was over tomorrow.'

After a few other pleasantries he hung up and the firelog burst into flame, and the four briquettes I mounted on top of it reddened in the stove. There's nothing I love more than going to my study very early in summer, when it's still chilly from the clear night, and lighting a token fire in the stove. It's a kind of ritual, like lighting candles before a service.

On the eastern wall of the room is my father's bookcase, in which I house my icons. The Christ of Sinai icon, from Belarus; the Madonna of Kazan, from Warsaw; the Colmcille icon, also from Belarus; these are hand-painted works of art by masters of the craft. The shelves are also replete with other images and icons of lesser significance as they are merely reproductions of originals: Saint Xenia of Petersburg, Rublev's Holy Trinity, Christ the Bridegroom, and a rare Russian icon of Sophia the Wisdom of God. And on my writing desk is a photograph of my wife.

Sitting on top of the writing bureau is the woofer for my Samsung soundbar, and on top of that is a golden Buddha which I brought home from a Tibetan monastery near Mongod in India. Above that hangs a painting of the Buddha Manjushri, and a photograph of the learned Tibetan lama who lives in west Cavan, the Reverend Panchen Ötrul Rinpoche.

If I could add something Islamic that might allow me to open my heart in that direction, I would have it, but so far I have not met the proper teacher to advise me, and for me religious objects are useful tools rather than ornaments.

No doubt someone might enter the room and be horrified by such an opulence of religiosity and such an overdose of deities from diverse religious traditions all sitting down together in the one space. But on the other hand you might come into my study and find none of these holy icons or objects on the walls at all; because very often I gather them reverently into boxes and hide them away in a press, or mask the glass doors of my father's bookcase with blue silk curtains to shield the icons from the world.

I do this when my faith has diminished, as it often does. And in complete devastation I just stare at the empty walls and view my faith with no more hope or optimism than a character in a play by Samuel Beckett; but when my hope and faith in metaphors returns I take them out and scatter them once again like flowers in springtime on the walls and on the many shelves.

They appear and disappear, as my faith ebbs and flows, and they reflect, I suppose, the nature of faith. It's not something that I can ever hold or make secure. It is not founded on any presumption about what is truth. But it comes and goes like the Atlantic tide on the long white beach at Carrickfinn in Donegal.

It struck me as I reflected on the phone call that perhaps the General was close to giving up the ghost. I felt that the abrasive comedy and scatological fire which fuelled him in the past was gone. He had sounded utterly dejected on the phone. Another two months of this confinement would be unbearable for him.

Perhaps I should phone him back. Assure him that August will come. That they will find a vaccine. That we will get together again, some day. And that if he could master Zoom and get his Wi-Fi sorted, then we might be able to have a laugh or indeed a drink some evening online which I knew he was well capable of, without the staff in the nursing home knowing what he was doing. But that would not convince him. When despair takes root in an old man's heart there is no rational remedy. Not even Covid-19 is as malignant as despair, and nothing is as susceptible to disease as an unloved heart. What the General urgently required was an embrace. From a grandchild, or partner, or just a decent friend. But he was bereft of them all and there was nothing I could do to soften that fact, by any pep talk on the phone. He would see through it and be further wounded by my condescension.

So I didn't phone him back.

For the first few years in Mullingar I felt displaced. In fact

the title of my column in *The Irish Times* was 'Displaced in Mullingar'. And I was. After ten years in a remote corner of rural Ireland I felt socially inadequate in Westmeath society, where conversations invariably focused on equestrian matters, and I was always left with nothing to say.

People got so involved with horses that in some houses closed-circuit TV was installed, so that guests could watch the newborn foals in the stables while eating their dinner. The foals in the stables lay down, or stood up, or ducked under their mothers' bellies to get milk, and everyone watched the black-and-white screens, with an intensity usually reserved for dramatic episodes of *Casualty*.

I remember one Sunday sitting through a supper of lamb chops without uttering a word. I was worried that the other guests might think I was depressed, and so to demonstrate that I was capable of frivolous chatter I mentioned that my cat had fleas.

The host stared at me as if I had just said that Joe Dolan was Chinese.

'Well, I don't think she has them anymore,' I continued, digging myself deeper into the hole. 'Last Friday I was eaten alive with them, in the bed; but I've had no bite since.'

I had an urge to scratch my beard, which I did without thinking; but as my fingers dug into the hairs beneath my chin, other guests glared at me in such horror that I feared they might ask me to leave. They didn't. But I left anyway, and went home to bed, and got bitten again.

It was around that time I first met the General. He stopped me in the Greville Arms one day as I was getting lunch.

'Are you the *Irish Times* man with the fleas?' he asked.

And then he laughed and explained how someone who was at the dinner party had told him the story. Back then he was always on the lake in May, and he'd phone me from his boat in the middle of Lough Ennell.

'My gilly is rowing as we speak,' he declared. 'You ought to be here.'

I was silent.

'For goodness' sake don't make a martyr of yourself,' he said. 'Is your prostate on the blink?'

'I beg your pardon?'

'The prostate,' he repeated. 'Is it acting up?'

I said, 'My prostate is perfectly fine.'

'Good,' he bellowed, 'delighted to hear it. A man over fifty should worry about nothing else in the world except his prostate; if that's shipshape, then all the rest is roses.'

Five years later my own prostate acted up so much that I passed a night in the bathroom screaming in pain, before being rushed to Mullingar Hospital where they relieved me with such delicate surgery that I was singing the praises of the health service for years afterwards.

But the General talked like that and there was nothing I enjoyed more than a morning stroll with him; to walk aimlessly around the busy town of Mullingar as the sunlight fell down on the narrow streets and shafts of it slanted through the windows of the Harbour Place Shopping Centre and a grey-haired musician outside the door played a mellow tin whistle that threw a rich soundtrack over the accidental buzz of all that town life.

The General strutted the streets like a loose bull, gawking at the silver-lipped teenagers, the struggling mothers, the screaming buggy babies, the tall-booted Slavs, and the little pot-bellied men who walked small dogs along the canal.

The General asserted that pot-bellied men so resemble monks carved on ancient monuments that one could not possibly resist the idea that such was the shape and size of the earliest inhabitants of this island. 'The Fir Bolg,' he would proclaim. 'The belly men.'

Some mornings the General and I took coffee in Café le Monde, or at lunchtime we might eat a bowl of Mamma Lingi's pasta on the corner of Grove Street and Blackhall Court. One day I asserted that Lingi's little parlour was almost as good as the wonderful Roma café on Bridge Street in Cavan.

'I have never been to Cavan,' the General replied rather dismissively.

Across the road Wisteria, a shop of posh fashion accessories, had a big 'Sale' sign in the window, and a man was coming out of Stars and Bows, – the hobby and craft shop – with a model of the *Titanic* under his arm, and to our left we could hear the laughter of women from the open door of the hair salon, Reflections.

We were eating slices of pizza on the street.

'This is delicious,' I said.

The General agreed. 'I have heard it said,' he told me, 'that sometimes the hairdresser orders slices for her clients, if they're a bit low on sugar or unhappy with their husbands.'

'Do you know,' he added, 'that a good hairdresser is better than a psychotherapist, although at this stage they're probably twice the price.'

We were staring at the boarding across the street. I wondered what was behind it.

He told me that that was where the archaeologists found the skeletons of twelfth-century monks a few years ago. 'There was a lot of pride in Mullingar when they found those monks,' he said. 'They had shells around their necks that showed that they had done pilgrimages to Spain. Mullingar was always European,' he added, wiping his lips.

Then his eyes darkened. 'Banana boxes,' he declared.

'I beg your pardon?'

'Banana boxes,' he repeated. 'That's how the holy monks left Mullingar. In banana boxes. After sleeping peacefully beneath the car park for eight hundred years, they were sent off to some storeroom in banana boxes. It was just no way to treat holy men.'

He was becoming emotionally volatile so I changed the subject. 'I think I might abandon my barber,' I declared.

'Why so?'

'Well,' I said, 'for a start, I never get offered a slice of pizza when I'm depressed. And the last time I was there he wanted to cut the hairs in my ears.'

'And did you let him?'

> 'That's how the holy monks left Mullingar. In banana boxes.'

'Of course I let him. How could I stop him?'

The General was horrified. 'You have gone far beyond the help of a hairdresser,' he said. 'You need a psychiatrist.'

'And there are machines nowadays,' he added, slightly embarrassed by the delicacy of the subject, 'for the ears.'

The relationship between me and the General was one of boy and man; me still a boy at fifty and him still a man at seventy.

And I couldn't imagine him being happy for a single moment without an argument.

But time passes. And in the turning of an eye I was in my late sixties and he was in his late eighties. The remembrance of him as an elderly but bullish mentor was no longer tenable.

He was infirm. His eyes were weak. His hand shook. And now in the time of the virus, as he looked out the window, all his might and prowess were gone. And he shrunk. I don't know how. So I couldn't dare to imagine what he was going through, in his armchair with a Foxford rug around his knees, during the lockdown. But as I remember him he swaggered ahead of me on the street, and was taller.

Or when he was still driving, I recall sitting in the back seat of his car clutching a briefcase on my way to Dublin. His niece was in the front seat.

'What's in the case?' his niece enquired.

'Nothing,' I admitted. 'I just carry it for comfort.'

The Dundrum Town Centre shopping emporium was ideal for a day out with the General; it was big enough for both of us to lose each other and thus I wouldn't ever know what he was up to. I went up and down the sloping escalators all afternoon, imagining myself in *Star Trek*, and was only mildly disappointed that I didn't get chatting to someone, the way I usually do in Mullingar.

But then I met Nancy, a white-haired old lady with sunken jaws and large spectacles, and as small as a bird. She talked to everyone along the mall and in the clothes shops. She was staring at the top shelf in the dairy section of the supermarket when I almost bumped into her.

'I don't like the Tesco milk,' she declared, as if she knew me. 'But I don't see any small cartons of Avonmore; are they up on that shelf?'

I reached up and took down a small carton of Champion milk. 'Will that do?'

'The bee's knees,' she said.

I met her again at the cold-meat counter, where she was getting slices of Denny's ham, and at the shelves of bread where she was looking for something high in fibre, and at the sweets, where she was trying to shovel jelly babies into a bag.

At the checkout I noticed little sachets of cat food in her basket. I said, 'My cat only eats the fancy stuff that the pet shop sells.'

She sized me up. 'You're a very educated man,' she declared.

'Why do you say that?'

'I can tell from the briefcase,' she said, laughing, and then she darted away down the mall, like a little sparrow.

Maybe I've always attracted old people's attention. Or maybe it's because I always knew that the older a person is, the more stories they have. Or maybe it's because I was always afraid of ageing and couldn't admit it to myself.

Such was the authority of the General twenty years ago that he could tell me how to brush my teeth and if I didn't do as he urged he would be offended. And when Osama bin Laden was shot by the Americans it was the General who explained it all to me: Osama bin Laden was merely following a rule of thumb known to all terrorists, that the best place to hide something is under the light. People might expect him to be in the dark caves of Afghanistan, but not in a big compound in a swanky suburb right beside a military base.

'Surely you remember that strategy from your own time along the border in Cavan. The IRA or any other terrorist group is familiar with the same tactics: hide yourself under a lamp. Am I not correct?'

He eyed me sideways like a crocodile.

'How would you know anything about the IRA?' I asked.

'I have my sources,' he puffed, 'in Northern Ireland.'

'What does that mean?' I wondered.

'Special Branch,' he whispered, with enormous reverence.

In fact the principle of hiding something in the most conspicuous place possible reminded me of a night long ago, during the Troubles. It was a snowy winter and I was drinking

> 'How would you know anything about the IRA?' I asked. 'I have my sources,' he puffed, 'in Northern Ireland'.

in a pub very late, while outside the hills were crawling with gardaí, and various armies, protecting us from gunmen, who were always trying to move weapons across the border.

When the last drinks had been served the late drinkers moved to the kitchen, as was the custom, and soaked up the alcohol with bacon sandwiches, and mugs of strong tea. Invariably the gossip was about cattle, sheep and the guns out there in the dark. And then an innocent question provoked a story.

'Did anyone hear that the Free State Army lost a man last night?'

No. Nobody had heard anything special. But everyone turned to the storyteller and waited.

The man with the story was tall and had black, oily hair and wore a long coat. He had big black eyebrows and smoked Sweet Afton cigarettes. He drove a Ford Cortina, and always carried bales of hay in the back seats for his cattle up on the mountains. A man of many sheep, a dog always beneath his seat, who could cross mountain ridges as lively as a buck goat. A man who knew more about the war outside the door than he was ever prepared to admit.

Snow fell in the yard, and we munched thick sandwiches and supped on sweet tea.

It was a new recruit that had been lost. A small, spectacled man out on his first patrol. His company had been deployed in a windy ditch on the snowy mountain, near where the gardaí usually set their checkpoints.

There being no traffic, the gardaí and army drove on to where a lonely farmhouse was tucked into the elbow of the road.

Dozens of cars were parked all around the farmhouse, which raised the sergeant's suspicions. So they stopped. The soldiers hopped into the ditch in the blinding snow and the sergeant went to the door of the house, half-expecting to find a bomb factory within. The door opened.

'Sergeant,' a black-robed widow declared, 'you're very welcome.'

The wake was in full swing and the widow presumed the policeman too had come to sympathise. Ireland is a small place and he was the local sergeant and he could hardly confess that he was there to search for AK-47s.

So he went in and took tea, and then a mouthful of whiskey, and agreed that the death was sudden, and that at seventy-eight her husband was not an old man.

Outside, the wind swept sleet across the mountain, flattening the rushes, and an hour passed before the sergeant emerged and hissed at his driver to get him home.

'Lord Jesus,' the widow exclaimed when she saw so many soldiers crawling out of ditches, 'it was very good of you all to come.'

The soldiers boarded the jeeps, and the convoy vanished into the swirling snow on its way back to base.

Back in barracks, the commanding officer realised he was a man short. So the convoy retraced its tracks in the snow and found one soldier in the ditch, gun at the ready still waiting for orders. He had poor eyesight and was completely deaf, and in the wind and snow he had neither heard nor seen his comrades leaving.

The tall man had finished his story and everyone agreed it was a blessing that the poor soldier had been found; they praised the sergeant for being so sensitive, and for paying his respects to the grieving widow.

'That widow is a fine lady,' someone muttered.

'Aye, she is,' another agreed, 'and she comes from a great republican family.'

'She does indeed,' a further voice affirmed, 'and wasn't her husband from across the border?'

'Oh he was, surely,' the tall man said.

'And where did they bury him?'

'Across the border,' the tall man said, smiling. 'There were checkpoints on both sides, but the hearse got through without any bother.'

I feel it's safe enough to tell stories like that now, because time has passed. Many of the participants are dead and gone, and the politics has changed, and stories don't cost lives the way they once did.

And I have thrived on gossip. I have made an art of rediscovering small stories. Finding in the meaningless meanderings of strangers, and other ordinary people, a kind of heroic failure, or faith in what is impossible.

In Mullingar the autumns arrived one after another, each one more swift

than the previous, dry and still, and the leaves around the big house in Shandonagh fell one by one as I stood admiring autumn colours in the oak trees with winter folding itself around me.

The General's robust bounce was faltering even then, and he no longer strode about with the haughty flamboyance of a turkey cock on the dung-heap that he once did in his fifties. The recession deepened its fingerprint in his bank books and he never quite recovered, and the gloom of a threadbare future gathered in his face, and he sat in a large, empty drawing room.

'Why don't you light a fire?' I asked him one time, but he couldn't be persuaded.

'It's been a while since I sat at a good fire,' he confessed. 'I'm trying to avoid using fuel until November.'

WHAT IS BEAUTIFUL IN THE SKY

We watched a Japanese movie that night. A slow-moving black-and-white meditation on the ordinariness of family life by Yasujiro Ozu, though it only made the General more miserable.

In the film a daughter asks her father was he in love when he married. 'At first we were not in love,' the father replied tenderly.

The General sighed in his armchair.

'But love grows in time,' the Japanese man said. 'It takes ten years to create this flower of love.'

'Bloody rubbish,' the General grunted. 'Fathers were not like that in the fifties, at least not in Ireland.'

He stared into the empty fire grate for a long time and when he spoke again it was in a whisper. 'When I was sixteen my father asked me was I gay. Of course he didn't say gay back in those days, he had another word for it. Basically I wasn't manly enough. And I think it was from that point onwards that I began to act more manly. And I joined the army. And I don't show my feelings; it's as if I wear a mask all the time. But as I get older I realise that the only thing left inside me is the ghost of a boy who never lived.'

During the lockdown I often think of nursing homes, and the splendid love and care my mother got in Newbrook in Mullingar. And I am ashamed to say that sometimes I am glad she died seven years ago and never knew the fears of living in a nursing home during this virus. Her generation had come through enough hard times without needing to be terrorised as they died.

I remember one time talking to a man in Delvin whose father fought in the First World War. 'My father was gassed in the trench,' he said. 'For years afterwards he suffered severe nose-bleeds. One day when I was five he fell in the yard, and other men ran to him, and there was blood everywhere. They were plugging his nose in an attempt to stop the bleeding; it was like a scene from a battle. They took him to Mullingar Hospital, where he died.'

'Was it a big funeral?' I wondered.

And one of the terribly mistaken presumptions that young people make is that by the time a person gets to seventy they have resolved their life.

'I don't know,' he said, 'because they never told me he was dead. In those days people thought it was better not to tell children anything.'

A few weeks afterwards, the little boy was in the yard with his mother, as she hung clothes on the line, and out of the blue the boy said, 'Mammy, why do you never wash Daddy's shirts anymore?'

She broke down in tears and told him that his father was dead, and that she was sorry for having kept it a secret from him.

And they were proud back then in the long ago. I recall another old woman telling me it was pride killed her husband.

'How so?' I wondered.

'Well,' she said, 'he went into hospital with a septic finger. It was just a bit of straw that had cut him. And it went bad. But he wouldn't stay in hospital. He insisted on coming home and then it got worse and he died. There was no point trying to talk to him.'

But there's an anonymity about nursing homes, a kind of grey wall behind which the unresolved lives of elders can be managed without their histories troubling anyone else. And one of the terribly mistaken presumptions that young people make is that by the time a person gets to seventy they have resolved their life.

Now when I went to visit the General, he was a cardigan of bones in my arms. Except that I might not see him again. I might never see him again if he was one of the unlucky ones during the virus's dark reach into the lives of the elderly.

Older people have their dreams and heartaches too; their anxieties and despair. They are as confused as the rest of the world about what is real or unreal and where heaven might be, or if it doesn't exist then why did anyone invent it.

When summer came to Mullingar the General was always at my side.

I remember lighting the first barbecue of the year on a Saturday evening, under the chestnut trees. The horses watched us from the field where the barley was harvested the previous year.

After the barley was gone, the pigeons feasted on the roadside for a few days, from what spilled off the trucks, and the barley fermented in their gullets and made them drunk, so they couldn't fly home, and a lot of them met their death under the wheels of oncoming traffic.

At the barbecue two musicians sipped beer before they began to play. The fiddle and the accordion were still in their boxes, leaning against a stone wall. The accordion player was unshaven and wore a greasy cap while the fiddle player was tall and dark, with joined eyebrows. They smoked leisurely, and discussed what age Mrs Hughes was when she died, the previous week.

'I think she was near ninety,' the old accordian player said.

Bridie Hughes played accordion in the Dinny Hughes Band many years ago. In the early days she and Dinny cycled to the venues – him on the saddle, and Mrs Hughes, sometimes pregnant, on the carrier seat, with an accordion strapped to her back.

'She was playing the piano in the house up until a few weeks ago,' the fiddle player remarked.

'She was fond of the bingo too,' the accoridan man added.

Then they went over to the wall, and tuned the instruments, and everyone gathered around the smoke, and plucked sausages from the grill. There were fillets of steak, for important people, and slices of shark for the vegetarian nurse, and teenagers grabbed the burgers, and everyone spilled salad dressing on their skirts and frocks and blouses and pants.

'Where are you from?' the fiddler asked.

'Arigna,' I said. 'But I was born in Cavan. In truth I don't know where I'm from. I am reasonably at home in Mullingar.'

'Arigna,' the greasy-capped accordion player remarked, 'is a lovely spot for music. Isn't O'Carolan buried somewhere up there?'

'He lies in Ballyfarnon,' I said, 'beside the lake.'

When O'Carolan was dying he made a final journey around the places he loved, calling at some of the houses he had filled with music over the years. At last he came to Mrs McDermott-Roe's door, in Ballyfarnon.

'I have come home to die,' he declared.

McDermott-Roe had cherished him as a child, and he now returned like a salmon, just in time to compose 'A Farewell To Music', and be buried in the land he loved.

He wasn't the only artist who loved the place he was born.

Liam O'Flaherty returned to Aran in old age, and kicked a big rock, saying, 'Aithním thú,' an Irish phrase that singularly expresses the mindfulness of one person towards another person; he was addressing the rock as a soul friend.

In comparison to the wounded hills of Leitrim, the streets of Mullingar were unnaturally jolly, and closer to Krakow than ancient Ireland. But after a few years I could feel a lovely

I once thought that Ireland might have buried its soul in cement, on the day the motorway was laid through the Skryne Valley between the ancient hills of Tara.

tug when I walked up the hill of Uisneach, or listened for ghosts whispering in the names of places; Kilbeggan, Kinnegad, Ballynacarrigy.

Unimportant villages in the sweep of history, but as places to call home they are no less beautiful than anywhere else.

The great novelist Kazantzakis was born in a village in Crete, where he played under the olive trees and watched cherries burst with juice in dark wooden buckets of brown water. And when he left home he carried a handful of clay in his pocket, just like the people of Tory Island in Donegal carry the clay of their island to the ends of the earth.

I once thought that Ireland might have buried its soul in cement, on the day the motorway was laid through the Skryne Valley between the ancient hills of Tara. Certainly some villages in Westmeath were almost buried in cement when the Celtic Tiger was leaping around in the first decade of the twenty-first century.

But by 2010 the young people at the barbecues across Ireland didn't care about Tara, or cement or new houses; and they did an enormous amount of hugging and kissing, because a few of them were heading for Australia on the morrow. History had swallowed them up.

Not just the boom, which vanished into air, and which people could cope with, but hugging and kissing and all that spontaneity that made us human has gone. And its loss changes us and has changed us so much that even now, only ten years after the time of the barbecues, it feels like another country. As the past always is. Though it lingers. The beauty of it.

My lovely General, in his stride, as he raised his brandy glass to the young people and sang for them: 'Landlord Fill the Flowing Cup'. Whether they liked it or not, he sang it.

As the evening closed in, the old people dissolved into shadows, the musicians put away their instruments, and the young ones on the patio set up amplifiers and monitors, and got ready to dance the night away, one last time.

I suppose beauty is what we reach for but never find. In our little destinies it eludes us. Or we are simply overtaken by age and time. But I like to look for something beautiful in a story. Because finding beauty or shaping the story around what is beautiful is always possible. Or at least was possible, before the virus came. I am always haunted by that image of the old monk in the boat, pointing at something beautiful in the sky with his finger, and the young monk in attendance following the direction of that finger and opening his gaze and feeling the kiss of moonlight on his skin.

And in the current mess of global chaos and the ugly face of a chronic lung disease it's not so easy to find. And it would be a disservice to the General to suggest that he is still out there somewhere huffing and puffing with an inflated ego, or swaggering around the streets of Mullingar.

He is old. And he misses the touch of humans he so long denied. The wife he abandoned, the children whose birthdays he so often forgot don't come to call on the old cocoon; so he is alone and in need. He calls me and I don't even return his calls because I can't see that it would do any good. I fail him every day.

So he cries in his nursing home, rubbing red eyes with the edge of his blanket. And I cannot pretend it is otherwise.

I sit upright for a moment and become mindful. Scanning my body with awareness. Scanning the room with awareness. It's going to be a good day. I will enjoy it even if I have to force myself. So I sit at the desk for a few moments, looking into the garden and enjoying the music of the birds outside as the sun rises higher over the mountain.

The fact is that music has always been fun. There was nothing really

quite like the wildness of a good session. Nothing more spontaneous than jigs and reels rising one after another, gradually, intuitively evolving, until the entire circle of musicians in some tiny pub were as one animal, singing, like a whale alone on the ocean's rim beyond Kerry. It was soul music. And joyful. And now it's gone.

I first met Martin Donohue – a big hairy musician – in the Farnham Arms Hotel in Cavan while I was eating my dinner. He was bald on top, but the back and sides of his cranium sprouted long brown locks that mixed with his big furry whiskers to make him resemble nothing else on earth. He was gazing at me through tiny spectacles as he declared that the Fleadh of 2011 would be 'the biggest traditional music festival in the world'.

'We're expecting over two hundred thousand throughout

the week, seventy thousand next Saturday alone. There's park and ride areas established at all entrances to the town. The Equestrian Centre has seventeen hundred tents. And everyone will be fed and watered. And all two hundred thousand of them will be walking up and down the street, in and out of the public houses, and enjoying the music.

'We're going to put a canopy over Main Street for all the crowds that will come to it; the All-Ireland Fleadh hits Cavan,' Martin declared. 'It's going to be big.'

Donohue's parents came from a rural background, a world where the only traffic was the footfall of friendly neighbours on the laneway or the remote sound of a post office van in the far distance, but they made a home for themselves on the Fair Green, a beautiful hill overlooking the town, widely known as the 'Half-Acre'.

'But I love this place,' Martin said, 'and I'm proud of Cavan. And we're going to bring the All-Ireland Fleadh back to the ordinary people.'

And he did. They did. On Saturday afternoon before the big opening, the phones were buzzing in the Courthouse, and twenty-two separate committees were finalising the last details, and Cavan seemed to be on the brink of a revolution.

There were sculptures everywhere – giants outside the Kilmore Hotel, a huge fiddle rising out of the ground at a roundabout, and canopies of steel and translucent fibreglass over Main Street, to protect the buskers and street musicians from the weather.

'It's a community celebration,' Donohue said. 'We're all in the music together. That's what it does. It brings us closer.'

He was so right.

'And the army base is accommodating set dancers. And Paul Brady is coming. And I got eight pianos, in tune, and put them in hotels, because people love a piano at night. They'll be squashed into every bar in the town.'

As a child I got faint intimations of Cavan's real musical heritage, when Seamus Fay, a man who was crowned All-Ireland lilting champion four times in the 1960s at the All-Ireland Fleadhs, and who drove our local bus, lilted reels and jigs as he was driving the bus into town every Saturday afternoon. The bus would stop outside our gate, and I'd take the lift into town for a haircut or to go to confession, as children did back then, and the sound of jigs and reels from the driver's mouth always astonished me. And I was seduced early, by the voices of old 'townies', whose terse south Ulster accents always seemed to be driven by cadences that were as tight as the notes in a hornpipe.

But the town kept a firm lid on traditional music, which in the days of gramophone societies and Gilbert and Sullivan musicals was not seen as respectable. Singing ballads in a public house was equated with drunken debauchery, and even poets that roved the streets with excessive exuberance were sneered at from behind closed curtains and dismissed as drunks. And the working-class people of the Half-Acre were shunned by the middle classes, simply because they were poor.

The All-Ireland Fleadhs that were held in Cavan between 2010 and 2012 changed all that. The passion and music and wit of ordinary folk blossomed. The Fleadh organisers and musicians had torn up the old image of Cavan, and they revelled for a week in one collective song of the soul.

On the final night of that first year, everyone gathered for the final session, in the old Town Hall, which had been a haven of music and other artistic endeavour in Cavan for almost a century.

'And you can expect a surge in the population,' Donohue joked. 'In '54 a lot of boys and girls were carrying on, on the bonnets of cars. That was at the first fleadh. It was a scandal. But I suppose there's more rooms available nowadays in the tourist trade, so we can expect a lot of Fleadh babies again next spring.'

And that's the way it went. There was music and fun, and you never knew where it led; you went with the flow and the joy of what happened, just as one tune followed another in a dance of living and loving. The Fleadh was always a place for intimate street life, for touching and holding and kissing.

I recall being at another Fleadh, with the daughter in August 2003, when she was nine years old. There were hundreds of people, shoulder to shoulder, holding hands, with musical instruments strapped to their backs, walking about the streets in the drizzle, just gawking at the world and each other; drinking coffee together in groups and talking about long-ago sessions, fingering knick-knacks at street stalls and admiring the glistening new instruments that were on sale in the shops. Teenagers on fiddles and concertinas, scattered about the streets, playing jigs and reels for television crews.

I bought my daughter a tin whistle and a CD of obscure flute music for myself, in the hope of learning a few new tunes during that winter. Even in 2003 I still had delusions about becoming a competent flute player. And I sat on a bench in the main square and chatted with a button accordion player.

'I had a bad summer,' he said. 'I was at the railway station one morning, on my way to the RDS, with two horse blankets. I only left them out of me hand for a minute, and when I came back they were gone.'

He stared across the street, to where three women in long dresses and brightly coloured scarves loitered, outside the post office.

Even in 2003 I still had delusions about becoming a competent flute player.

'But it was the pheasants that really broke me heart,' he explained.

I remembered walking his land in early May, to admire the tidy coop he had built in a sheltered hollow for the little brown birds; over one hundred of them, strutting about behind wire mesh, and surrounded by an electric fence that would burn the snout off any predator.

The fox had slaughtered over a dozen before he put up the fence, but when I viewed the coop he was optimistic about the future; it looked as secure as Guantanamo Bay.

'But they're all gone now,' he declared. 'Every one of them.'

I said the fox must have had wire cutters, and an enormous appetite.

'No,' he said, 'it wasn't the fox, it was the rain; I went away for a week and when I came back they had all drowned. I never thought that a sandpit would hold that measure of water.'

He winced.

I assembled my black flute and played a tune, to cheer him up. But even music cannot lighten the heart of a man who has lost seventy pheasants in one night.

And then two women standing near the post office decided to join us; Romanian women in long skirts and headscarves. Again we touched shoulders. Shook hands. Admired each other as humans do, without ever imagining the world any differently.

I played a tune as the youngest one danced; a teenager in a long brown dress and a sky-blue blouse and a black frock-length waistcoat. Her young face was encased in a green scarf, and realising that my friend was not happy she sat beside him, and linked his arm, and made him smile by leaning her head on his shoulder.

Then a third Romanian woman appeared out of the crowd; she was also young, but looked gaunt and delicate, and she wore a sheepskin coat with fur at the rim, like the ones that used to hang on the top of stalls in the Dandelion Market on Stephen's Green years ago.

The tune I had played was called 'My Darling Is Asleep', and when the gaunt woman heard this she came over to me and said that she was a widow. 'My darling is asleep,' she repeated, slowly, and embraced me in a gesture of affection, and I felt her heart beat inside her as I held her.

They moved off like birds as suddenly as they had come, slipping through the crowd as nifty as swallows through the air.

But just then I noticed John Daly, a fiddle player from Mallow, sitting outside a coffee shop across the street, and Pádraig Sweeney, one of Roscommon's finest flute players, strolling towards us, and Art Duffy from Derry at the door of a music shop clutching a new Odyssey flute in its silver case. It was only two o'clock, and the last lovely afternoon of summer was about to begin.

Those were easy things to bring to mind. Easy to write about. They were like tunes that just travel into the universe. It's like you put the bow to the strings and out it all flows. You put your lips to the wooden flute and the breath seems to come through you, up from the ground, out from the lungs and into the cylinder of rosewood. Or you put your arms around a stranger and the perfume of otherness creates a place where you can dream.

Music is the food of love and the

fragrance of love, the promise of heaven in every breeze. But when my daughter went away to Australia with a young lad from Donegal on a dry autumn afternoon in September of 2019, silence crept into every room. They packed their bags one Sunday night and we drove them to the airport on Monday evening.

She didn't show emotion in the car, other than excitement at the thought of heading to Moscow that night, and Bangkok the following day, and eventually to a new life in Melbourne.

I didn't show emotion either. I sorted all that out in the garden on the day after they left, when there was no one to see me cry, and no witnesses other than the trees to know how I felt.

The garden was always a refuge; an acre of oak and birch around the house, in a sloping field on the side of a hill. And it was quiet on Sunday, apart from a few cars in the distance, heading towards church in Arigna.

I put petrol in the lawnmower, pulled the starting cord and the machine coughed into life.

It made a hum like a small motorbike, and it soothed me as I manoeuvred around the trees and along the ditches of high grass.

It's a hum that drowns out all else. It rinses the heart with a clean, single-pointed calm. It slices the demons of negativity in little pieces, as the ferocious blades flail the grass.

Mowing grass had always been a consolation to me. I can picture slow Saturday afternoons as a child, when the little suburban lawns outside Cavan, dainty as manicured fingernails, all hummed with the same high-pitched screams of baby lawnmowers – as if everyone was in pain and the only release was to waddle around the garden behind a mowing machine and allow it to do the screaming.

But over the years the lawnmower became my ally. Its hum often made a blanket for my sorrow. The sound of it gave me something to hold onto, like a monk gripping his mantra with single-pointed attention.

So there I was on a quiet autumn afternoon, following a machine for two hours as it walked me around old memories.

Like the tree my mother gave me when the child was christened. The rose bush that came from a garden in Clare where my father once lived. The bay tree Tom MacIntyre sent. And the wild rose my beloved planted on my sixtieth birthday.

Not to mention the little rose the child planted herself, and the box hedge she trained the dog to jump across like a racehorse when she was seven.

A garden is like a novel, full of memories, and storylines and emotions I'm still living through.

The big chestnut was a wedding present; we kept it in a pot for four years, until we found the right spot for it. And nobody knows who planted the Chilean beech trees, although by the size of them I reckon it may have been an archangel.

Beneath the trees and in all the ditches there are numerous ornaments and old relics that were lost over the years.

I found the old sweeping brush she used as a jump for the dog when she was training him to be a racehorse.

I found a tennis ball in the weeds. And a wooden trolley in a ditch which she used as a child in winter to shift snow. I found the old sweeping brush she used as a jump for the dog when she was training him to be a racehorse.

And I was shocked to find the swing, still intact, hidden among the pines – the red plastic seat faded and the blue ropes frayed to their last few threads. It brought to my mind another long-ago autumn day, when I watched her sitting on it, with a satchel on her back as she waited for the school bus to take her off to her first full day of education.

The trees hold me; their branches nurture me more effectively than the arms of a good mother. Sometimes they are like a cathedral of impermanence: in summer they burst with birdsong and in winter all the dead leaf rustles with hidden life beneath my feet. But only in autumn do they go silent, as if they were frightened of death.

By the end of the week the daughter had begun her new life in Australia. I went out one morning, sat on the swing and rocked gently in the still air. I intended cutting the ropes and throwing the old plastic seat in the recycling, but there's something about an empty swing that is untouchable; and there's an absence in it, which nothing can cure.

And that's where silence creeps in and stories die. Because it's too hard to talk about sorrow. If stories are the music then sorrow is the space between the notes. The silence out of which grows each melody and into which every last song finally falls back, and fades away, and is forgotten.

Every tune comes out of silence. But sometimes there is only silence. Like a full stop. And that's what the spring of 2020 feels like to me.

A pause that is not a pause. And it's not possible to go backwards.

The week after she left, myself and the beloved were in the kitchen, looking at the empty nest for the first time. OK, she had been living in Donegal for a few years, but that was like being down the road. Australia was another world. And she was gone. And we were alone. You can feel it, right? The silence of the little kitchen. But what did we even know of silence back then, before the masks, and the respirators, the social distancing and the hand gels and the garda checkpoint on the road into Carrick-on-Shannon to ensure we all stayed in our houses, and in particular the elderly cocooners, who got spoken of in the third person more than any other group.

They were to stay at home and out of the way during the lockdown. I suppose it was a good and caring policy, but its implementation was devastating for clusters of lonely old folk who were watching their friends in nursing homes getting trollied off for burial one day after the next.

Last year, I was sitting behind two old men in a hospital waiting room when

I was attending coronary care clinics. It was a large, crowded ER with rows of country people lined up for various consultants. People hugged children with swollen legs, or bandaged fingers, or cut heads. But the two gents, skeletal thin, in dark suits and caps, were calm and content in the cluster of squealing babies, while nurses from every continent on earth rushed to and fro with little bottles. The old men might as well have been waiting for a bus on the first day of their holidays in Salthill.

They were arguing about a woman.

'I have it to say,' declared one, 'that I talked to a woman who lived through the Famine.'

'That's impossible,' said his comrade.

'I'm telling you, she was a hundred and four when she died.'

'Sure she had a son far older than you.'

'No.'

'She had.'

'Alright. She had. But he was seventy-four at the time. He was drawing the pension at the time. In fact they were both drawing the pension at the time, mother and son. I met him too, if you want to know.'

'How could that be?'

'He lived with her.'

'I know that.'

'She was one hundred and four when she died. I have a photograph of her. I have it to say I spoke to that woman. She was alive in the time of the Famine. She was a hundred years of age then. She got the money from Doctor Douglas Hyde, and it was presented to her by the parish priest, and I have the photograph.'

More facts returned to his mind.

'I even remember the funeral,' he said. 'And right underneath where the house used to be, you know the turn that they called the Narrow Elbow?'

'I do.'

'Well,' he said, 'on that hill there was thirteen cocks of hay when she died. And there's only trees growing in it now.'

They were silent, as they brought some field in the long-ago bog of memory to their minds. They were as still as monks enveloped in prayer. And I couldn't figure out what might ail them. The lungs perhaps? Or the heart? Or maybe cancer?

I worried that they were so engaged in conversation, they might miss their turn in the queue because they were sitting very close to all the women with new babies.

'When did she die?' the doubting one enquired. 'What year?'

'Nineteen and forty-two,' said the other. 'She was a hundred years of age, in thirty-eight. Doctor Douglas Hyde sent her the money, and the parish priest presented it.'

The case appeared to be closed. Except that his comrade had a bombshell.

'I met her myself.'

'Ye did not!'

'Oh I did. We were looking for stray sheep, as boys, and when we saw her we had to go in for tae. The people were very generous in that time. You'd be brought in for tae; very generous.'

'Oh that's true,' the other one agreed, though he was deflated, and he swiped the air with his cap as if trying to hit a fly. Then he began singing:

> Now the ship she sails in half an hour,
> Across the broad Atlantic;
> My friends are standing by the Quay ...'

A pregnant woman, in a blue dress, with black hair tied in pigtails and carrying an infant, approached the boys. I thought she was going to give off about the singing.

'Are ye done?' says one of them to her.

'Yes,' says she.

'Right then,' says the other gent, 'we'll get you home.'

It was my turn to face the doctor, as the three of them, with their infant, went out the door and back to the bogs beyond Killucan.

I am not uneasy in hospitals. I have often spoken of my life as a night porter when I was a teenager – fetching glasses of water in the middle of the night for old men with lung disease, emptying aluminium nightjars from under their beds in the male ward each morning, measuring the urine in fluid ounces and writing the results on their charts.

One of my beech trees came from an island in Lough Allen. I took the sapling home in a boat after making a visit there with an old miner twenty years ago.

Wheeling bodies to the mortuary on steel trolleys – through the maternity unit and out into the back yard in the middle of the night, so that pregnant women wouldn't be distressed as they queued for their morning showers.

In rural Ireland old people are everywhere. Over the hill. Up the road. Sometimes standing at the crossroads waiting for the social service bus to take them into the day centre. And every year in Arigna another old miner is carried in a coffin to the graveyard and another well of story and memory about the extraordinary life of coal miners in Arigna is dried up forever and the untold stories are buried. And I am ashamed at how much I have ignored them.

One of my beech trees came from an island in Lough Allen. I took the sapling home in a boat after making a visit there with an old miner twenty years ago.

He recalled two old ladies who lived on the island when he was a youth. One harsh winter, infirmity forced the women into nursing care on the mainland, he said. After they left, he landed on the island to peep in the windows where their nightclothes still hung above the kitchen range and he poked about in the debris of the abandoned house where the ladies had lived since their childhood – a time when the ferryman was summoned from Drumshanbo by the gong of a giant bell on the island.

The miner was old, breathlessness betraying disease in his lungs, and he wasn't given to exaggerations, or wasting words, so I believed him when he told me that on the day he went to the island he was attacked by two swans, and that ever since he could not look at swans without remembering the two ladies. After the miner died I used to see a hawk, regularly, hovering above the island and I often wondered was that him.

It's been three months since I last stood in Dublin at a Samaritans

event, among all the volunteers, and celebrities, including Mary Kennedy who spoke movingly about her life, and Philly McMahon, a Dublin footballer who spoke about the damage that drugs did to the lives of people in his family. I met an old friend from the theatre and chatted about how swiftly time passes.

'When are you going to write another play?' she wondered.

'Life slips by,' I replied, 'and we drift in directions that we never planned.'

Although the impermanence of theatre was its attraction. It was an illusion. When two characters kissed and fell in love on stage, the moment was as beautiful as it was fleeting. It disintegrated. It had no permanence. It mirrored life because in life nothing lasts.

I left Dublin City Hall alone and walked up Dame Street to

the hotel where I was staying across from Christchurch. The hotel was in shadows, but the walls of the cathedral across the road were lit up.

I was thinking about an evening I stood there many years ago with a group of schoolchildren from Fermanagh. We had come to attend a Taizé prayer service, an hour and a half of chanting in the packed cathedral, while the tiny figure of Brother Roger dressed in white robes, abbot of the monastery at Taizé, knelt before the altar. He was the perfect image of an elderly man. He had lived through war, seen the futility of it, and dedicated his life to reconciliation, love and prayer. Now he was small and frail and white-haired but there was an aura of strength in him that grew out of his kindness.

Afterwards I ploughed through the crowd to make a path for my young students from Fermanagh so they could get close to him. When I got to his petite body I whispered in his ear. 'These young people have come from Northern Ireland to see you.'

He turned to them immediately, and paid them complete attention, embracing everyone so that they wept with awe and excitement, and I too got a chance to embrace him as he looked me in the eye and I felt naked.

His presence stayed with me, long after that night. Even after his own demise, brutally stabbed to death on the altar of his own monastery. Life is short.

Who can know what the virus will bring? Maybe the overall outcome will be good, I hope. Maybe rituals are the only way we have to make the invisible visible – and to manifest something permanent in an impermanent world.

In the spring of 2020 I went through old hard drives, photographs

and letters from the dead, and shivered at the person I had become, and the person I was before the virus. It seems like I am never who I think I am, either then or now. The footprints I make on the earth always turn out to be footprints of a stranger.

Sometimes I wake in the morning and my beloved is still asleep. I rise and walk about the house, and then around the garden, trying to enter another day in lockdown without screaming.

I go to the kitchen and check the time. The clock says 6 a.m. I sit at the table, and accidentally squash my reading glasses under my arse. The day is off to a bad start. And I'm stressed.

'But I won't let the virus win,' I whisper. 'Nor will I allow the lockdown to depress me.'

With headphones I listen randomly to stuff in my music

library. 'The Deer's Cry' by Arvo Pärt. John Moriarty talking about how humans got disconnected from the evolving cosmos and went their own way, thus bringing the planet to the sorry impasse of unbridled capitalism, pollution and the confinement we are now enduring.

I put coffee in the pot and leave it on the hot ring until the water bursts up the funnel and I harvest a tidy little cup of tar-like liquid.

Sometimes I take this coffee to my studio to meditate or pray. But there are other mornings when my faith doesn't survive the night and being mindful is like trying to hold smoke in a saucer. I am devastated from the moment I wake. I feel like a detective in a book I haven't read – a meaningless speck of an indifferent universe.

I'd like to be in harmony with nature. I'm a writer. But I don't burn with zeal, as great writers often do. I'm lazy and uncertain. Even starting the day with a positive attitude can be tricky.

I'd like to be as the geese are, that fly over me, or like the dolphin is, that slips through the waters shaping her: the force of the sea or the wind carving their beauty across millions of years.

But I'm not a dolphin or a goose, just a human overreaching himself with expectations, over-anxious about a tiny virus and helpless in this newly locked-up world.

Eventually the only thing I can do is take some coffee to the beloved. I open the curtains. Tell her it's morning. Present the hot cup. I return to the sheets and in the privacy of our home I hug her.

As it happens I am aware that this hug will become the

richest part of the day. It is the portal through which I slip into an interior landscape where all is well and will be well; where dolphins and geese sing in harmony; where Arvo Pärt and John Moriarty hold hands and dance.

The tenderness of a hug is almost perfect – apart from being slightly tarnished by the knowledge that there are many who cannot find a hug anywhere. Many who might search

> The tenderness of a hug is almost perfect – apart from being slightly tarnished by the knowledge that there are many who cannot find a hug anywhere.

every drawer in the house, change all the clothes in the hot press twenty times a day and paint the fence blue, but not a hug will they get.

I know one particular lady in her eighties who lives alone. Her husband is dead, and she misses him – but she also misses life as it was before the lockdown.

She sends me occasional emails, but it's as if she was waving from an island at some passing ship in the hope of catching their attention; I stand with indifference on the ship's deck and watch her.

Before the lockdown she went to mass, received the host from a Eucharistic minister's hand, and sliced many scones to share with her best friend in a coffee shop on the way home.

Even in Dunnes Stores she used to bump against other people, and feel the touch of the young cashiers' fingers as she paid for her groceries; and as the cashier passed the change back into her palm, counting the euros and the twenty-cent pieces, cent by tiny cent.

A hairdresser would call to her house each week. It wasn't that she needed her hair perfectly shaped in silver-blue locks, but the accidental touch of the hairdresser's fingers kneading her scalp made a difference.

And there are stories of others, who have been forced to endure their final hours on earth with only an iPad to touch, a screen of pixels to run their finger across, in tiny acts of tenderness and farewell.

One evening I made a shrine for an artist who died. I sat on the patio with candles and a black-and-white image of her, thinking about how we will all cross the same river eventually, and praying that the angels would lead her into paradise.

One morning I stood for ages at the window staring out at the desolate fields and the deserted road. Days regularly passed like that during the lockdown as I moved about in a private universe and the beloved beside me moved in hers. Then some accident required we pay each other attention for a moment.

'What are you doing?' the beloved asked.

But I couldn't tell; I felt like a dazed rabbit that had been hit by a tractor and just managed to get home to his burrow.

'And why are you wearing that peaked cap in the kitchen?' she wondered.

The fact was that my peaked cap had begun to stick to my head. It happens to a man when he turns sixty-five – a mysterious glue of psychic attachment prevents the cap from coming off, even when he is eating his dinner. Some men are stuck to their caps for so long that if they took them off nobody would recognise them.

'Take it off,' the beloved said one morning, suddenly exasperated.

'Take what off?' I wondered, thinking she might have sex on her mind, but she only meant the cap.

In the lockdown I feel a ruination I never imagined. Deeper than depression, or physical burnout. Because this is ontological. And even though I have lost nobody directly to the disease itself, it's strange how anxiety created by the virus overwhelms me and I brood more and more about people long ago gone to death. Giants of love and wisdom who would have been consoling to speak with on the phone or in a Zoom meeting, if they were still alive.

Of course the philosopher and poet John O'Donohue is one of the more obvious giants that was lost far too young, and sometimes when I imagine what it would be like to talk to him in this crisis I find it hard to believe that he died over a decade ago. A philosopher from west Clare who was eloquent and wise and articulate. I imagine his insights would be an amazing consolation at this time.

WHAT IS BEAUTIFUL IN THE SKY

We were in the seminary together, in the same class studying theology, and we took a lift to Italy together in a truck in the summer of '82 a few weeks after we had both been ordained as priests. We went over the top of the Alps, and stopped at an old church near Mont Cenis, where a caretaker greeted us, in the fog and snow, and brought us into the ancient sanctuary.

There we saw a splendid altar, on which stood two majestic candlesticks. The caretaker said that Napoleon had come across the snowy path on one occasion and rested there. When he returned to Paris he sent the candlesticks as a gesture of his gratitude.

John fingered them with love; it was the way he touched everything he came in contact with: the flowers of the Burren in County Clare, the rocky fields of Connemara, and the hearts of all the people he met around the world, through his writings.

In Milan we had a few drinks with the truck driver, bade him farewell, and then got a train to Venice. We stayed in a monastery where the abbot was an expert on Caravaggio, and the monks put brandy on their ice-cream in the refectory every Sunday.

Just before his death, in the winter of 2007/8, John was in New York and he went to a concert in the Lincoln Center where a violinist was playing a Tchaikovsky concerto in D.

He had a single seat near the front. He was so close to the young musician that he could feel the intensity in her body as she played. She was so alive in the passionate and creative act of making music that he wept. It was the measure of how intensely John O'Donohue loved life, and how he had continued, all his days, to be fired by awe and a reverence for beauty.

He told the story to an interviewer from National Public Radio, but by the time the interview was broadcast the following month John had been laid to rest in the cold, damp clay of a graveyard in Clare.

His work inspires me and his presence haunts me beautifully, but there are times in this isolation when it is hard not to imagine how better it would be if he could write this book, or if we could once again saunter across the bridge in Maynooth from the old seminary to the new campus and idle one more afternoon, with a few cups of coffee, and sing the praises of Tony O'Malley, Kierkegaard and John Moriarty.

John O'Donohue was never at the Joe Mooney School,

a week-long festival of traditional Irish music, song and dance held in Drumshanbo every year in the third week of July, but I think he would have loved it. Berry's Tavern packed with fiddles, flutes and a bouzouki. The style was furious. Musicians with red faces sweated over their instruments like men at the hay. I recognised one tune as 'The Battering Ram'. Then I recognised an American woman I'd met before.

I said, 'Let's go down the street to Monica's Pub, it might be quieter.'

It wasn't. Beneath a low ceiling two uileann pipers, one accordion player, two concertina players and four fiddlers were clustered in harmony, flailing away at the polkas, and it struck me that when uileann pipers dominate a session the music tends to sound less furious, and more medieval. They open out a delicate baroque structure at the core of each tune.

The piping in Monica's was like a soundtrack to a European banquet somewhere in the sixteenth century.

In the afternoons, when the morning workshops were over, I would often step inside someone's house and sit at their table and shake their hand or embrace them in the kitchen without any reason apart from the fact that I hadn't seen them since yesterday.

Paddy McManus, a publican on High Street, and a building contractor who had done renovations on the house I was living in, sat in his armchair in the kitchen on Saturday evening, as contented as a large cat, when I stepped in unannounced, while his wife Betty fried a pan of boxty. It was the last evening of the festival. Outside the streets were quiet, and the pubs were swept and sparkling, ready for the final sessions. The world was holding its breath for the sun to set and the night to begin.

Forty-nine tutors had given classes in twelve different instruments to hundreds of musicians from across the globe, and each night the pubs hummed with a single language. I thanked Betty for the boxty and headed down High Street.

The High Street in Drumshanbo has an elevated promenade that links the public houses, and humans of every gender, race and age were wandering around with instruments strapped to their backs. People shared chips and beers, and sat on the wall.

'We still have the photographs of you from last year,' one tall German man joked with a local.

'Aye,' said the local, 'so do the guards.'

A Hungarian man pinned me to the wall telling me that the Tuatha Dé Danann came to Ireland in a flying ship, but

WHAT IS BEAUTIFUL IN THE SKY

could not land as the Fomorians had set up an energy field that they could not penetrate. So they had to circle nine times before finding a breach in the energy field.

'That is why they landed their boats on top of Sliabh an Iarainn,' he said. 'Did you know that?'

'It's the first I heard of it,' I said, 'but thanks for telling me.'

'I'm Irish-American,' she pointed out. 'Fair enough,' I said, 'and no doubt you feel like an exile and you long to find a home.'

An American lady told me that she was in a nightclub in Basel recently where they had bowls of condoms and earplugs on the counters. I said, 'It's an education just listening to a well-travelled American.'

'I'm Irish-American,' she pointed out.

'Fair enough,' I said, 'and no doubt you feel like an exile and you long to find a home.'

'I guess we're always looking for home,' she replied.

And it's true. Every year they down tools every year and walk away from their desks and tune up their banjos and arrive like old fish at the top of the Shannon, because music offers them a kind of home, a refuge. They're just ordinary people – teachers, painters, plumbers – and sometimes they come from tattered lives where they no longer feel at home. But in this place they can shelter and immerse themselves in a tai chi of jig and reel, as their collective psyche shifts into a different zone, where they find it. They find home.

'But I don't play an instrument,' the American said.

'Neither do I,' I replied, 'but I'm an evangelist for the flute. And I believe reels and jigs have a rhythm as hypnotic and calming as the chanting of Tibetan monks. And music is the real language of all Ireland. Remember that in the big houses of ancient days Irish may have been spoken in the kitchen and English in the parlour, but everyone danced to the same tunes.'

I ordered us another drink. The only thing on the counter was a bowl of peanuts.

'Come back next year and try a workshop,' I suggested. 'You can't imagine the pleasure of spending an entire morning learning a single tune and then playing it all afternoon like a contented child.'

'I used to play the tin whistle,' she confessed. 'Do you think it's too late to find one?'

'Now you're talking,' I said. 'I know a woman down the street who has an entire handbag of them.'

And on it went as if forever. Smiling and laughing and touching, and passing one tin whistle from my lips to her lips and her lips to some stranger's lips, all for the joy of another tune, and relishing the expressions of love and seduction in every open face. Forever young and the bars never closed, and nobody would have ever imagined us in surgical masks that would wipe the smile off a corpse.

It's almost 9 a.m.; time to take a break from reading the script. I go to the house and find my beloved already at breakfast. I toss some porridge oats into a bowl and swamp them with water, and place the bowl in the microwave.

I sit at the table. We have nothing to discuss this early. We both enjoy the silence of morning. And besides the seventh of June is like the sixth, and the fifth, and all the days that went before, right back to the twelfth of March when I first realised we were facing this long period of retreat.

Just over eighteen months previously a stent had been inserted into one of my arteries and my beloved had her own slight health issues that made us both nervous. So we phone a list of groceries into Declan in the Gala Shop once a week, and when he has them packed I drive down in the van, and he comes with everything in a trolley to the car park and I pay by credit card.

The beloved and I have guarded each other from shallow, random conversations that scatter the mind's serenity too suddenly in the early morning. We avoid the news. The papers. The politics. I try not to bitch about the president of America, the prime minister of Britain or the strong men of Europe. It's a loving silence. We wash our bowls like individual monks in a monastery. We go our separate ways for the day.

Each of us has enough to think and wonder about.

The daughter arrived one afternoon, just before April when the lockdown was made official, although we had been observing it since March 12.

She came to the garden. We stood at a distance. Then she went away, this time to England, to find work. It had been a grim winter without her when she was in Melbourne. Her return to Ireland was a joy. But she is young, and needs a life, and so she went again.

I spent a lot of time in the camper van, with the heater on, during the coldest months of winter, sitting in the rear and looking out the darkened glass windows. I'd listen to magpies in the high spruce tree. They have become our friends simply because they have endured over thirty-five years up there in the branches. One generation after another.

I can talk to them.

I ask them do they have children in Australia or London.

And their cries break the silence, and the wind breaks the silence, and all the noises of the woodland and the screeching storms are beautiful in my ear.

Because it's a talking universe. The landscape speaks.

So it's not just up to me anymore to chatter, write or talk. I can sit in the back of the camper van and listen.

I love winter. The days shortening. The beloved walking around the yard wondering where I am because the van windows are dark and she can't see in.

I thought winter was an appropriate time for such isolation. I thought by March we would be up the road in the camper van heading for the sand dunes of Carrickfinn.

The hardest things to write about are personal tragedies. It feels

inappropriate to intrude on private pain. And suicide is so intimate and personal. But burying the dead is not a private act in rural Ireland. It's like a collective hug. It's a ritual during which physical closeness is fundamental to the communal expression of grief. An entire parish squeezed into some little church and gathered around the broken mourners, draped in black clothes, as they sit frozen and bewildered in the front pews. The grief is public even when the deceased is another young man fallen victim to the demons of depression.

There was one particular funeral the previous autumn which was a devastating blow to the entire community around me. It wasn't long after the daughter had gone to Australia, and when I drove up to the local church in Arigna there was a huge crowd outside standing in the rain, waiting for the hearse to arrive with the remains of the man who had died.

Or maybe I should call him a boy; because he was only days away from his twenty-first birthday when he went out alone on a wet Thursday night intending never to come home.

He was a young farmer, who loved his sheep and was out and about on the land no matter what the weather. An ordinary country man who could be seen often in Drumshanbo Mart on Thursday evenings, or in the pub at the weekends, expansive and cheerful with his companions.

And though he had suffered from depression he didn't ignore it. He talked about it. And he was even man enough to get help. To go to the doctor. To go to the hospital in Sligo, realising that he had developed suicidal ideation. Some say the hospital should have kept him in longer. Some say they should have paid more attention to the risks he presented. I don't know. But it's a pity that like so many other victims of suicide, he simply fell through the net of care and love that was around him.

He was only a boy – a child, eager to live. He learned to walk before he was two years old. He always wanted to be a farmer. He had a girlfriend whom he cherished, and he missed his father, who had died some years earlier.

But yet who can measure the terror the comes in the night when someone falls into depression? The fear that grows in the swampland of the soul, when demons of negativity and despondency afflict a human being.

Like hundreds of others in rural Ireland every year, he was so frightened of the dark that in the end he could only think of surrendering to it. And like a frightened child, he even told people about what he feared would happen. And then it happened. He would have been twenty-one on the following Tuesday but they arranged the funeral for Monday, so that his mother wouldn't be forced to bury him on his birthday.

Just after communion a young, slim youth, a friend of the deceased, stood up and positioned himself right in front of the altar, facing the coffin, and sang his heart out.

He had no accompaniment, and his voice negotiated the melodies like a sean-nós singer, drawing as much meaning from the phrases as was possible.

I watch television dramas depict rural Ireland as a dystopian nightmare, but I want to shout at the screen that it's not like that. It should not be like that.

He sang Leonard Cohen's 'Hallelujah', and 'Raglan Road', and finally he rendered 'Amazing Grace' with such raw personal emotion that the congregation applauded.

The priests put away the communion bowls in the tabernacle and in the ensuing silence I could feel the peace that often surfaces in the aftermath of a meaningful ritual.

It lashed rain in the churchyard and the oak coffin was splattered so fiercely that one devout lady whispered in my ear that she felt the Mother of God was in the vicinity, weeping for her own child. Such is the lyrical imagination of country folk.

Neighbours stood around and young boys and girls cried and one old man with white hair looked stoically at the grey clouds.

'He had the makings of a fine man,' he said.

'It's a terrible thing,' I replied.

But he just nodded and said, 'But sure that's life.'

And it's true. In rural Ireland, that's life; funerals are part and parcel of every ordinary day. There are graveyards in Leitrim, Mayo and Roscommon, and on the edges of every small town in Ireland, that open wide the earth for such weekly tragedies, and where people cling to each other in the face of death's conundrum.

People wonder why so many lovely boys lose the war with depression, and why so many mothers are robbed of the joy that comes from small things – like birthday cakes and parties, and warm, tight hugs – things that this dead boy can never do again. But there is no adequate answer. And not even an entire church of mourners can compensate a mother for that loss.

So I shook their hands and walked away. Drove off up the hills and perched the camper van on the edge of Scardan Waterfall, with a view of Lough Allen and the mountain beyond. Where can I go, I wondered, to find something beautiful in the sky.

Scardan is a lovely word. It doesn't exactly translate as

waterfall. I'm told it can mean the cloud of spray that comes off a fall of water when the wind blows. So I was told one day in Donegal by a native Irish speaker.

'It's a lovely word,' I said to him.

'Aye,' he said, 'it is.'

He was very dark. Big black brows and a tuft of raven hair across eyes that made me think he had been a hawk in a former life.

'It's a beautiful language,' I added.

'Sure there you are,' he said.

I watch television dramas depict rural Ireland as a dystopian nightmare, but I want to shout at the screen that it's not like that. It should not be like that.

And then I go out in the real world under the real sky and wonder if it is me that's wrong. If faith and hope and love are mere delusions of the brain. That's the kind of darkness that comes to me in this isolation and lockdown.

And if that's how miserable I am, then what kind of darkness is the General ploughing through, I wonder.

Every evening since the twelfth of March I met the beloved in the

television lounge. We watched the news to get the daily report of deaths and new cases from the disease.

'We go live now to our health correspondent,' the anchor-woman says, and then he appears on screen, impeccably dressed, with dark coat, a fancy tie and a clean fresh shirt. He understands the gravity of his daily task. He knows what it is to announce five hundred more deaths in a single day.

Every death is a catastrophe. Every death is the ending of the cosmos. But there was one death that affected me more than others. And it happened not on account of Covid, but months before the virus arrived. It happened not as a result of illness or tragedy but in the natural course of events, as the final completion of a life in old age. And as beautiful as a leaf falling, he fell. That was the only way I could describe the death of the poet Tom MacIntyre.

I could feel a silence inside me, like a tiny virus, hardly noticeable but growing from the moment he took his last breath. A silence that could swallow me.

It was in 2019, a long-ago time, before the virus robbed mourners of their grief and ritual. A long-ago time when there were all sorts of services and sermons and rituals and crowded churches.

Before corpses were numbered in body bags, or shifted in sealed coffins out of sight by masked undertakers and whisked away in unmarked vans, as some broken old man or woman cried out at the gable of a hospital morgue, watching the van pull away with their deceased love en route to a lonely grave.

Tom MacIntyre was lucky. He lived long and died well in his bed, with the comforting touch of his loved ones through every second of those last days, journeying with him to the very edge of the abyss. And he had three priests on the altar at his funeral and the president of Ireland in the front row. A pageant rich in ritual and poetry that befitted his stature as a poet.

But I was bereft. I was stunned by his death. The loss that opened in me was enormous. Only when he closed his eyes for the last time did I fully recognise the implications that he had been my mentor for forty-five years.

For about the last year of his life he had been quiet and composed on the pillow, dreaming his dreams of death. Getting lost in the fog of his own memories. At one stage he surfaced to greet his beloved with a smile and said to her, 'I'm falling into some tricky spaces now.'

For the rest of the time he was cheerful, gracious, but still, as if listening for something. And anyone who attended his bedside felt he was leading us not into a great silence but to somewhere across the river to the mythic land of non-being. His death was like the opening of the first curtain at the beginning of a grand opera, or one of his own exquisitely poetic dramas.

At least that's how I imagined it. And I played him tunes on the flute about a year before the end. Six months to go and I just sat across the table from his beloved and spoke to her about the poetry of faith and belief, as he sat at the top of the table, reading from his diaries. Every so often he would raise his head and see me as if for the first time.

'Wonderful that you could come,' he declared. Repeating the words later when he saw me again. Over and over he saw me for the first time. Declared his enthusiasm. And returned to the page, the word, the fog and the dream.

Coming close to the end I sang for him at the bedside, a few phrases of the song 'Red is the Rose.'

When I was finished he looked at me as clear as when we first met, and said, 'That's a very old one.'

And he seemed pleased. And I was startled that he had come out of the woods, the fog, the void, to break the silence, to speak again, and to be with all of us in great lucidity for that final week.

'How are you doing?' I asked him.

He smiled and said, 'I'm attending to my prayers.'

It's something he had said over and over again, through the years. Admonishing me so many times with that same injunction: Attend to your prayers.

Not that he meant it in a conventional sense. He was a man

who acknowledged the expression of love in all religions, but didn't have much time for any particular one. And I'm not superstitious in a narrow sense, but it was very strange and beautiful how a book belonging to him fell off a shelf in my studio the night he died. It was a book of poetry by Rumi, which MacIntyre had given me as a present some years earlier.

Beautiful, because MacIntyre himself used to relish reminding me that there are no accidents. Everything is a sign if we use it wisely.

He attested to the sense that everything that needs to happen will happen. That you can rely on the universe to reveal what is necessary. And all we need to do is respond with love.

Nobody had a voice like him and when he spoke I fell in love with him. And when he wrote poems I felt he was carving something beautiful in the silence; he was sculpting in time, as Tarkovsky might say. Singing the universe into existence. Saying what is unsaid.

I had no such pretensions about my own craft. All I could do as a writer was listen to others – remembering what they said and repeating it. I told other people's stories.

Echo.

For example, I spoke to a young woman in the chipper, one Saturday night, whose face glowed with joy. She was working behind the counter, dipping my chips in oil.

'You look extremely cheerful,' I said. 'What's the reason?'

'I've just been accepted for a course in university, to study Egyptology,' she told me, as she handed me a plastic container of curried chips. Clearly Egyptology is what she wanted in life, and when she got it, it made her happy. Her joy had a cause and foundation.

On the other hand, my joy sometimes arrives without reason. It appears as an architecture of my emotion but without any foundation.

One Monday morning in the month of February 2020 I was standing at the front door, wondering who to vote for, and looking at two blackbirds playing on the lawn, when bliss overpowered me like an emotional rash.

The lovely birds filled me with such contentment that I sat on the step dreaming of a perfect world where there are no tears, and I dearly wished that I could vote for that.

The blackbirds played on the lawn for about ten minutes, waddling to the right, and then to the left, while the sound of Anna Netrebko singing on my computer wafted out the door and blended with the birdsong.

Then a jeep rumbled up the road, and a politician stopped and stood before me, offering me his photograph, but initially I ignored him.

I was paralysed by the blackbirds, and in comparison to my inner joy, all external phenomena, including the local candidate, appeared to be nothing more than an illusion. Just like the statue of Saint Teresa in her ecstasy, by Bernini, I had been transfixed by bliss.

The sound of the candidate's jeep faded in the distance, and I waited for another sound, or anything that might assure me that I still had a foot in the real world. But no sound came from the road, and I took the absence of traffic as a sign; the stillness was like a door into some 'elsewhere', a whispered clue of the infinite presence behind the veil of the ordinary. The lockdown was only weeks away. It was already in full swing in Wuhan. But we were even then oblivious. I was in Warsaw all through January, with fog on the streets and ice on the pavements, and most coffee houses deserted except for myself. The Christmas lights still twinkled in the dusk each evening and the nights were long as I sat alone in my apartment.

Although I loved the apartment – a huge open space with floor-to-ceiling glass walls overlooking the street. I had a small desk in one corner where I wrote for hours interspersed with long walks around the city I had come to love in winter.

The lockdown was only weeks away. It was already in full swing in Wuhan.

Apart from those ominous dispatches from Wuhan on various television stations there was nothing to bother me.

At night I dreamed more than usual of my childhood and of the days I wandered around Donegal as a teenager, along the edge of the bog, half in love with ghosts and blackbirds and the silhouettes of fishermen coming home from the sea.

And like all dreams the narratives were mixed and confused, conflated and illogical, and I always woke with a strangely uneasy feeling, as if something was being said in the dream that I missed. As if I wasn't listening closely enough.

As if the tolling bell from Wuhan, issuing out in news reports every evening, was inducing in my dreams a kind of private ecstasy of things remembered, a joy and exuberance for a life that had already been lived.

I returned to Ireland at the beginning of February and as I faced the grim reality of the polling booth at the end of that week to vote in the general election, I felt I was marking my X for a world that would never make me happy.

There was no point in telling anybody that if I could, I would have voted for blackbirds, and ghosts that fish in the night and light fires in the dark, rather than for any of the political candidates on my list.

I would vote for music too. For life as a long session where everyone stands in summer clothes, and touches each other, with elbows and arms and fingers. Circles of musicians clattering away without end. Where everyone embraces each other at the end of the night, and some go off to make love until dawn on hills where all knowledge is as easily available as an apple; because love is a kind of knowing.

Like it used to be everywhere in Ireland, no matter where I went, on any given day of summer: on streets and in the little cosy lounges, where tourists and visitors and local musicians shared in one single unifying trance of joy. It's what we used to do. It was called having a few tunes. It was called passing the time. It was called a session. A céilí. A day out. A night in. A bit of craic. And fun. We called it all life and we thought it was normal. Until the virus put a stop to our gallop.

I was at the music summer school on Achill Island in 2015, on

the pier, thinking about MacIntyre. I had once taken a lift in a boat from the same pier to visit the poet on Inisbofin. I stood for a long time facing the wind until a flute player touched my shoulder.

'I haven't seen you since the day we met in Drumshanbo,' he said, 'the year I ate the rope' – meaning the year he separated from his wife.

He whisked me away from my daydreams and we both went to a bar full of men in working boots, drinking pints and watching the races from Galway.

In the lounge, children with musical instruments were getting ready for a competition called 'Hata Acla'.

I hadn't a clue what 'Hata Acla' meant, but the flute player explained.

'Once upon a time there was a special hat in Achill,' he

said. 'It hung on a post near the mainland. If anyone was heading away, and had no hat of their own, they could take this hat as they were going off the island and return it when they came back.'

A lovely myth – as if Achill was a little family in a little house, and the road around the world was only a day's walk, and anyone could be home before dark.

In the lounge two microphone stands were arranged on a small stage. Two girls with hair parted on the right side, and clipped on the left with pink hairclips in an old-fashioned style, played concertina and whistle. The softness of their hornpipes was unbearably beautiful.

Another contestant had tied a cuddly toy to the neck of her harp for good luck.

A boy in a Mayo jersey gulped Lucozade from a bottle at his feet before he delivered a song his grandmother might have sung as she washed her sheets, or his grandfather might have lilted while making nets.

The children of Achill have been forced to hang their hats in far-off lands through many centuries, yet they hold this music in their hearts as they ride the subways through grim worlds they have not yet imagined.

A German woman gave me directions to Dugort. As a child, she had to travel eight hours to find the sea.

'But I live in Achill now,' she said, and she smiled as only those in love can smile.

That afternoon I headed west, towards Croaghaun mountain, and the finest cliffs in Europe.

I passed the church, where thirty years earlier I had

witnessed a moving funeral rite. Three young boys had been taken from the sea, and laid out in coffins, side by side, as a bishop sprinkled holy water on the oak lids, and relations outside hugged the hearses and wailed their sorrow at the sky. That was the day I waited at the pier until I got a lift to Boffin. The boatmen had been in Achill for the funeral.

In 2015 I zig-zagged around the whitewashed walls of Toblerone holiday houses that had been built in the meantime, and through a desolate bog, where a cluster of Traveller vans and trailers were tucked away from the wind, and far away from the gaze of settled folk.

Finally I arrived beneath the slopes where, sixty-five years earlier, an RAF plane crashed in thick fog, killing eight servicemen on board. Bits of the engines were still up there sunk in the earth.

In Gielty's Bar later a circle of musicians, young and old, sat in the corner, rattling out tunes and songs that will continue to be sung for many more years into the future, when the old singers that walk now are dead and gone, and the young ones are turning grey in the suburbs of American cities.

The following morning as I ate breakfast in the guesthouse I watched a plumber in a blue van, copper piping lashed to the roof, dropping his daughter off at the school down the street, for the workshops. She struggled across the windy yard and up the steps with her fiddle case. The wind was hammering the New Zealand flax on the ditches.

A woman in the breakfast room beside me watched wistfully, and said, 'I have a daughter in America, but she is illegal. She can never come home. On Patrick's Day, when the bands from all the villages are assembled in Achill, I do call her, and hold my mobile phone up in the air, so that the sound of the pipes and drums can travel across the ocean to her apartment in Boston, where she hangs her hat and makes a home. She loves to hear the music from Achill.' Perhaps, as MacIntyre used to say when he was being expansive at the dinner table, 'Complete beauty only visits us in solitude.' Perhaps getting to the heart of the matter means getting to that secret room inside the heart.

In 1993 I lived in a small bungalow in east Galway, surrounded by flat fields near the village of Skehana. I would often cycle to a mausoleum in Monivea, and gaze in a cracked window at two coffins that lay side by side, festooned with ancient sashes and covered in dust.

Locals said that the mausoleum was built for Robert ffrench, a diplomat who married a Russian princess in the nineteenth century. I spent many afternoons loitering around that mausoleum, meditating on the splendours of marriage, the shortness of life, and the fact that we all end up in separate boxes.

I spent other afternoons sitting by the Stanley range in the kitchen of my rented bungalow, gazing out the window at the empty road, waiting anxiously for my beloved to arrive from Dublin, on Burkesbus. I would bake sweet rice in the oven, for no other reason except that sweet rice was a source of comfort to me in childhood.

My mother used to leave a pot of milky rice coated with

sugar in the oven until a brown skin on top indicated that it was well baked. I looked forward to it on winter days after walking from school, my shoulders hurting from the straps of the schoolbag and my face hurting from the sting of the wind and the humiliations of the day.

Years later, when our daughter was young we went to Enniscrone on a holiday. Because of the weather I spent three days on a balcony overlooking the beach, drinking glasses of

> I would bake sweet rice in the oven, for no other reason except that sweet rice was a source of comfort to me in childhood.

brandy and gazing into the Atlantic. There was a lot of drizzle, and rough winds, and I staggered around the beach in a haze of ozone, like a character out of the book *Death in Venice*.

Finally, halfway through the first week of the vacation, I headed for Ballina in desperation, and bought a few fresh buns, which cheered me up. I planned to consume them that evening, with the beloved and the daughter on the balcony perhaps, sipping café royale, and wrapped in blankets.

For lunch I had fish and chips in a restaurant near the

river, as sheets of rain carried paper bags around the streets, and the staff kept the door closed in case the wind might ruffle the hairs of little old ladies sipping tea.

One waitress told me that she had intended going to Lidl that morning to buy a tent. She put her alarm on for 7 a.m., knowing that only the early birds in Lidl get any bargains.

'But goodness me,' she said, 'I slept until a quarter past eleven, and I had to be at work by twelve.'

'You've had a hectic morning,' I suggested.

'I know,' she said. 'Sure didn't I go upstairs a few minutes ago and I could still see the track of the sheets across me face.'

I glanced at her, and sure enough a little red line crossed her forehead and cheek, and brought the two of us into an endearing intimacy that I would have enjoyed extending for the rest of the day had she not been so busy.

I was tempted to crown the meal with a bowl of rice pudding, but the waitress returned before I was finished my chips and said that she had an ice-cream on the shelf that no one wanted, and if I wished, I could have it.

She carried it to me on a tray, a mountain of red syrup dripping down the white slopes, and I felt that people were staring at me as I sunk my spoon into it.

I returned to Enniscrone in the late afternoon and went straight to the beach. White waves clapped down at my feet, each with the sound of distant thunder, and a salty hurricane lashed my face.

I passed children in wetsuits, with surfboards under their oxters, staring at the waves like a line of ducks, and a young couple pushing a buggy at high speed. I passed a father kicking ball with his son, and three teenage girls in swimwear squealing in the waves. Close to the water's edge two old ladies were holding their hats, and a bull of a man, in swimming togs, was jogging. I passed two men with a giant kite who were unravelling its strings with the gravity of engineers handling electricity cables.

A rope across the sand marked the limit of the lifeguard's territory, and beyond that I was alone. I leaned into the wind, and I walked on for a long time.

At the beginning of April

in 2020 I got some of the chairs that usually remain idle on the patio and placed four of them in different locations around the garden. One at the very edge of the cliff, hidden by a clump of bramble, so that I could sit there without even the beloved knowing where I was – a complete solitude overlooking a cliff. A second one I placed on the east side of a beech tree that had been cut into a bush, and was thick enough for robins to nest in and for me to sit behind and be out of view from anywhere in the garden. If the postman came, as he did each morning, he would not see me behind the beech hedge.

With leftover tiles from the time we made the patio I constructed solid ground under the trees in the very depth of the woodland, where I could smell the garlic as it grew, and there I placed the other two chairs.

This morning I was at the cliff when I got a text from the beloved. It was about 11 a.m.

Where are you?
In the garden.
I can't see you.
I'm down at the edge.
Coffee?
Be up in a minute.

Another respite. Be careful, I cautioned myself, not to speak too much. If I talk too much in these conditions I release too many ideas and then the ideas infest my mind like fleas in a bed all day.

So up I went, and into the kitchen. She had made two coffees in glass mugs – true percolated coffee from fresh beans and then mixed with warm milk from the microwave.

'How are the cats?' I wondered.

The cats were a good subject of conversation. It was light and cheerful. Not too complicated with emotion. No danger of leaving a residue of dark thought in the mind afterwards. The beloved works hard at her sculpture. But her studio is at the extreme south of the property, behind the woodland. It is beyond everything. It is her world – an other world. She goes there and works. She creates her sculptures. That's all I know. And the independence of her realm and mine has provided us with space within the space, and lives within the single life that marriage is.

We often like to talk about the cats. They are like children. They are like us. They are empty vases into which we can pour our loves and sorrows and the fruits of our imagination.

And now I am in my studio again. The cats are on the

water tank licking each other and enjoying the sun.

So that went well. A good coffee break. No unnecessary ideas bumping around in my mind like bees in a jammer.

The cats are wonderful companions to each other. The big black tom was born in a neighbour's house, but he fled, perhaps from having been badly treated, and he went wild. There he met the real wild one, a little tubby and thickly coated male with bad eyesight.

The big black tom might never have survived two entire winters in the wild without his companion. When they first appeared at our door I was afraid to touch either of them. They were both feral and aggressive. But gradually the black one remembered its childhood and grew tame and domestic again and ended up on the sofa.

The other one, a black-and-white warrior, has never come inside. Instead he remains wild, but devoted to his companion every hour of the day. In the evening the two of them come to the patio door. I allow the black one in. I invite his companion to come in too.

But he doesn't come. He remains at the glass door, staring in, watching his beloved for half an hour, as if to be assured that his companion is OK. And then he vanishes for the night.

In the morning both are outside, because the black one goes out very early to urinate. So both have their noses to the glass of the bedroom window by 7 a.m.

I open the window. The black one enters. He sweeps down onto the floor and straight towards the kitchen with his tail high in the air.

I follow.

But instead of waiting for his food, he goes out again through the flap, drawing me with him, and so he stands, now outside again, with his companion, awaiting their breakfast.

They don't let each other down; the black one will not eat without his companion.

The coffee at 11 a.m. was great and I went back down to the edge near the cliff and sat there a while longer as the two cats followed me. They began to play, and their playfulness in the grass had the opposite effect on me.

They made me feel like I should be working. I have more to read. More script to examine. More stories to sign off on if I am to close this book today and get to the end of everything.

I have a memory of MacIntyre in his forties, his long,

ivory fingers adorned with turquoise and ebony stones on elegant rings. Holding a glass of wine. His white hair flowing down to his shoulders, to the wild colours of his knitted jumper.

A fish in the oven.

A knock on the door.

Another guest.

Another night of conversation.

He was a poet. His words were doorways into heaven. He could make the invisible visible.

He wasn't an alienated soul. He was a native Gaelic poet, even if he wrote mostly in English.

He was a shaman, a lightning rod. A ghost from the first day we met. He sang all the ballads at street corners on Fair Days in my imagination, and on a long bench at the foot of every corpse in the wake house of my soul, he keened. He kept alive the flame of my heart's sovereignty. He turned dinner conversations into ructions. He followed the caravans of love wherever they went. And his dinner parties were high-octane events.

He demanded and commanded attention.

He wasn't everyone's cup of tea. But for me he was a light.

And I needed to give him so much attention, that I forgot myself. He was like the kestrel hovering over the cliff. The blackbird in the garden. I looked out the window to see him and for an instant I forgot who I was or even that I existed. A person can draw you out of yourself. When you are focused on them you forget everything else. That's one of the biggest pieces of wisdom I ever learned. If you get that idea, then heaven is instantly available. You don't even have to wait. It's here now.

There was a time in west Cavan when people firmly believed in heaven. They would sing a hymn entitled 'Going Home' at the door of the church as the coffin was wheeled out into the wind on a trolley, along the uneven path of weeds and stones to the graveyard on the hill.

Old men at the cemetery gate would joke about what the theological implications might be if a coffin fell off the trolley. The sods clattered on the coffin lid. The diggers continued and people listened for the blade of the shovel hitting some stone or an ancestor's skull as the grave was finally closed in.

But those sounds, of shovel in clay and stones on the coffin lid, clattering in the hole below our feet, called us beyond the pale moon of morning. The very sounds, or perhaps the silence between the sounds, implied something deeper in the still air – a sheltering place more true than death, and nobody was embarrassed to believe in it and call it heaven. The universe was limitless in its possibilities back then.

I believed in heaven and still do. Anyone who ever sat under the hawthorn on the hills above Lough Allen, watching Sliabh an Iarainn turn red at sunset, or listened to bats at evening time come out to feast and clap their wings around the sky above the smoking barbecue, knew well that there was, perhaps not another life, but an alternative life – a way of walking more deeply on the earth, as Moriarty would say. That there was a hope at the heart of everything. That there was a beauty in the sky. That you could choose either the poetry of being here or the unbearable anxiety of being here.

Nobody would wish for a world where someone might die alone, in a hospital ward. Where the only way they might be able to say farewell before they were intubated was to wave a last farewell on an iPad. Their body taken to the cemetery with grim precautions by undertakers wearing face masks, and antiseptic sprays lying on every car seat, with burials conducted in haste and the grave closed over immediately. And all this being the narrative told over and over in heart-wrenching videos that families were forced to share through the internet so that children far away in America or Australia could share a little of the grief.

But yet it was at those same lonely mortuaries, and in those isolated graveyards and on those grainy iPad screens that the real and extraordinary story of Covid-19 was played out.

Because the love that binds human beings is a force not

measured in digital data nor the quality of a sound system in a graveyard. And the people who died in that time were not alone in their dying.

Love is a union, a shared experience that makes us human, and no amount of plastic masks or isolation curtains or locked doors or glass walls can stop love transforming everything and everyone.

Whatever splendid heaven may shimmer beneath the

> They say young love is an accident. When the time, place and circumstances are right people just fall in love.

surface of the material world is not some place from which humanity can be barred or excluded by any quarantine.

They say young love is an accident. When the time, place and circumstances are right people just fall in love. They may plan a weekend together and nothing more, but by Sunday evening they may find that they have been swept off their feet. They proclaim that they are in love, and their destiny has been sealed in a single kiss.

Of course it's not accidental. The universe unfolds with a shape and form and necessity all of its own. Love gathers individuals up into a bigger picture and demands that they live out the destiny that was planned for them at the beginning of time.

What I learned in the lockdown each evening as I watched the unfolding of almost two thousand deaths was that love still gathers so many into one.

Young love is strong, but it's only after many decades that people realise love never dies, and that no matter what colour the mountain or how dark the night we are never alone when we are loved.

The crowds in the church at MacIntyre's funeral mass were immense – standing outside, and packed into the pews, grieving and praying and singing and clapping, and none of them would have imagined what was coming. We had time to believe in heaven back then.

MacIntyre didn't just believe in heaven. He insisted on somehow inhabiting heaven, even if he was only crossing the street. And even the cremation of his material remains couldn't deprive me of the conviction that the light of heaven would forever shine on him.

His wife recited one of his poems about a beekeeper: how the widow must tell the bees that the beekeeper has died. She stood to speak the poem before the coffin where it rested on a plinth just inside the open curtains.

As the beekeeper's widow speaks, the bees begin to swarm and in the swarm the widow sees the figure of the lost beekeeper.

But as the poet's widow spoke the poem I saw MacIntyre's ghost, invisible yet imaginable, walk towards her one last time.

Cremation didn't feel right. It was as if the attempt to dissolve his body and soul into air before our eyes had misfired. MacIntyre stepped out of the coffin before the final curtain and moved like a cloud and disappeared out the door and down the road in the direction of Bailieboro. Clearly he too was heading home.

But even his death could not be denied. Because where there was once a compass point, now there was nothing. This happens with parents; when the second parent dies, the child knows how close death is. For me MacIntyre's death had that effect. The wish to write anything further drained away.

I met a theatre director at the funeral.

'We must get you back into the theatre,' he said. 'You must write something new for us.'

I said, 'I have nothing more to write. I am almost sixty-seven. I just want to live by the ocean now.'

Did I say that? Did I actually say that to the director? I can't quite remember. I don't think so. I think I said yes, sure, we should meet, but I'm not in Dublin very often. That's what I said.

I said something bland. I don't think I actually articulated what was in my heart.

I am almost sixty-seven now. I just want to live by the ocean.

The Atlantic roars against the rocks for thousands of miles along the Irish coastline. It's been in my ears since I was a child. But now in the lockdown, after seventy days, I hear its waves singing all the time in my heart. Day and night. I cannot silence it.

When I was younger writing exhilarated me. And even now when I close the door of my studio and light the stove and sit at my desk I still get some pleasure. But for shorter periods of time. And there are other things now that make me just as happy. Like playing with the cat, or watching the magpies having an argument.

It's 11.30 a.m. and I am losing my concentration. I put the book down and stoke the fire in the stove. I throw on six briquettes. I know it's too much but I can't resist it. This is summer, but I want a plentitude of heat around me. I sit in the armchair and rock myself a little.

I remember frosty mornings on the streets of Mullingar when I first began

writing for *The Irish Times*. Red-nosed people were heading for work and the canal was frozen solid beneath a cloudless sky and I was almost unable to restrain my joy at being alive. So many folk beginning their day: heading to work or exercising their dogs. A time when their hearts belonged entirely to the morning. And I belonged to them. Loving them just by passing them on the pathway, so that then I could return to the big house in Shandonagh where I was living, just outside the town, and light a fire in the study of that nineteenth-century farmhouse and write – the entire day stretched ahead of me as I sat at the desk, with sun slanting in the window and the fire at my back.

It was amazing to have found an audience through the *Irish Times* column, although I had not yet realised that my dislocation from home in Leitrim would also bring depression, illness, and finally a long, slow recovery in the hills above Lough Allen ten years later.

But everything that happened me in life has been nothing more than fresh material for more storytelling. Whether it was religious ecstasy or existential depression or the small emotional devastations of every ordinary day, to me it was all rich when lived again as memory and story. And this was especially true in Mullingar during those five years from 2006 onwards, when I was surrounded by so many others with their own amazing tales to tell. I could write their stories, their faces, their expressions and their pet dogs into columns in private acts of love.

Best of all were the little intimacies that happened when someone spoke to me on the street or in a shop doorway. I wrote it down and lived it again, relishing its magic twice over. Writing was an exuberance. I was never much good at writing out of sorrow or taking revenge on the past in the stories I called to mind. When I was depressed I played the flute, and I cooked a lot.

I made a lot of pancakes, apple tarts and buns. The preparation of food was a ritual that anchored me deep in the cosmos. Just like sweeping the floor of a meditation room, cooking can empty the mind.

In Mongolia they used to tell a story about sweeping the floor. Once upon a time there was a student who wanted to study with a great teacher. But the teacher thought he was too stupid to learn, so he just allowed him to clean his prayer room. For a lifetime the simple student swept the room, with his eyes fixed on all the sacred objects and statues of the

Buddha. In that simple way he became enlightened. His unfortunate teacher, so the story goes, took many more lifetimes without making much progress.

It was only once that I couldn't write at all. I had a severe case of writer's block during the Celtic boom and it sustained itself on and off during the financial crash. The only way I could free my mind of distractions during those times was when I cooked.

Mixing margarine and flour to make pastry. Using Golden Delicious apples and spicing them with a pinch of cinnamon and a handful of cloves. Mixing butter and sugar on the pan, adding water, and drenching the apples with sweet juice before covering the tray with a final layer of pastry.

Oh Mammy, Mammy, Mammy, I intoned, I remember you.

In the beginning I cooked a tart almost every day, and devoured it by night. And it was around that time I went to the doctor for a check-up.

'You're eating too many apple tarts,' he said. 'Your cholesterol is gone up. If you keep eating apple tarts the cholesterol will go through the roof.'

I told him that I needed to cook in order to write. 'It's only when I relax that I can actually sit at the desktop and put sentences on the screen. What will I do if I stop making tarts? How will I write?'

He shrugged his shoulders. 'I'm not a writer,' he said. 'I can't answer you on that one. I'm a doctor and your cholesterol is high. That's all.'

And here again is an example of how a casual conversation can endure for years as the turning point of a story. How a stranger can slip into the narrative and mark a moment of significance. The visit to the doctor was inconsequential at the time. But looking back, it was a clear warning sign that I ignored. So the doctor's presence sits in the book as a representation of all the times I never listened. In hindsight, he showed me how deaf I was to others.

And now I sit at my desk thinking about him as if he were still in the room. Then I raise my head and look at the icons. Christ stares back at me but he is never smiling. I don't know of any icon in which the Christ, historical or cosmic, servant, bride or lord of the universe, is ever smiling. That's a pity.

I fall almost entirely into sleep, at the fire, and dream of lunch. I'm sitting at a table with a white tablecloth and Christ is behind me whispering in my ear.

'I'm smiling all the time,' he says.

His voice wakes me. It's almost noon. And I'm hungry.

My mother expressed her love through cooking. It's how she shared. I've written about her tarts and buns so often that I once received a letter from a woman in Dublin describing to me in great detail how to make almond buns identical to the ones my mother used to make.

First she made the pastry. Then she put on a layer of apricot and syrup. And on top of that she sprinkled almonds, finely chopped. All this was baked on a moderate heat for thirty minutes.

So how could a woman in Dublin know all this? I wondered.

Then I read on:

Long before you were born your mother showed a young girl in the neighbourhood how to bake those almond buns. And that girl grew up and continued making those buns all her life. And now that girl is writing this letter to you.

I rise from my armchair and connect to Spotify. The deep voices of monks in the Russian monastery of Valaam draw out a single note as they begin their hymn. I sit back at the fire. Faith is so beautiful and comforting that I wonder why it took me so long to accept it. Why I couldn't see that religion was always a form of psychotherapy. And nothing more. Just another way of being here, now, in this present moment. The icons are only a lens. The figures in my imagination are only a lens. They are a focus through which I can see the present moment and walk in the real world.

I suppose I'm a slow learner, as my teachers observed when I was a child.

I always ate compulsively. I fed myself anxiety. As if all that food, the buns and spuds and tarts and ham and sweet rice pudding would ease some pain I was unconscious of.

The poet's meals were the only exceptions. MacIntyre demanded attention. And if you didn't give it he could sense something was wrong.

'Why am I thinking you're not enthused by this conversation?' he might ask as we discussed the grandeur of wild flowers or the verses of Caoineadh Airt Uí Laoghaire.

'Your heart is not in it,' he might add.

So I had to put my heart into every moment with him.

When he lived alone by Lough Sheelin, and went into the woods near the lake every evening at dusk to gather kindling for his fire, I would arrive on the dot of six. We would dine formally on fish, fruit and perhaps some coffee. He never gorged. He took his food like a zen priest. Each mouthful was medicinal. I think he would have delighted in this lockdown. To know that each long day could offer so much stillness that foxes come again to the back doors of town houses and fish jump so high in the Cavan lakes that people mistake them for birds.

That's the kind of sentence he might have written in his relish for heaven's shimmering silence, which was an accidental consequence of the lockdown. And of course MacIntyre never drove a car; he told me once that he was against them on theological grounds.

It's half twelve and I'm still thinking of food.

There was nothing I wouldn't eat when I was young. Chips. Indian takeaways. Legs of turkey. Bread puddings. Potatoes. Steaks. Chicken. Chicken legs and chilli chickens. Boxty. Eggs. And potato cakes. I put berries on porridge. I put ginger in tea. Cinnamon in whiskey.

But I'm so hungry now that I'm getting a headache.

When I was young nothing bothered me at all. Even underwear didn't bother me. I could wear any old vest, T-shirt or string top that was lying around the floor. I would walk the summer lanes with as much bare skin exposed as was decent, and at night I never wore pyjamas.

I slept in sleeping bags, in confined spaces, with other boys – behind couches, in the back of old vans, or in tiny tents. I embraced the world with cocky enthusiasm, and even at night I swaggered when I got up to pee, moving about in the moonlight with the affectation of an untamed wolf. Or so I supposed.

But there was no wolf in me, just someone who wanted to belong; and as boys we all belonged to each other, like a pack of hyenas. Life was never lonely back then, and I could not

To know that each long day could offer so much stillness that foxes come again to the back doors of town houses and fish jump so high in the Cavan lakes that people mistake them for birds.

have imagined the labyrinth of solitude that a middle-aged man can stumble into as he mooches about Dunnes Stores, trying to find pyjamas and thermal long johns.

My middle age was spent in places like Café le Monde in Mullingar, even then still comforting myself with food like enormous buns.

I used to meet Daniella there, a tall, sallow-skinned Italian woman, who studied art and design, and spoke six languages, and had remarkable eyes, which she decorated with lashings of eyeliner. She was weeping into her coffee one morning because she could not find a watch to send to her father for his birthday.

'Surely there are lots of lovely watches in Mullingar.'

'Yes,' she agreed, 'but not the Rolex I am looking for.'

'A Rolex would be very expensive,' I said. 'Perhaps you should buy something cheaper.'

'Of course it is expensive,' she said, with indignation, 'but he is my father.'

She wanted to know what was in my bag. I thought that would be too much information for a young lady.

'Groceries,' I lied.

She picked up the bag and laughed when she saw the long johns and the paisley-pattern pyjamas.

A blackbird outside the window warbles. It makes me shiver because the door is open and he sounds so close. It blends with the monks from Valaam still reaching low notes as they chant praise to God in Russian; I cannot understand the words but I can feel it.

And Christ of Sinai is still gazing out at me from the bookcase. There is a space opening. A space where nothing happens, only waiting.

And the waiting becomes vast and full of song. Suddenly I hear the car pulling out and I know that the beloved has just driven away.

One night in the Abbey Theatre

I was watching Mike Scott flitting about the stage, like a spider with long hair, and Steve Wickham, a dark presence in a Venetian mask, making the fiddle talk like a cormorant. They stretched the poems of Yeats to the ends of the earth, and I fell into the well of their magic.

As I listened to Mike Scott singing Yeats I got the feeling that there are no dead people at all, and that heaven is just around the corner where all the poets and musicians of the past are dancing behind a veil.

And of all the fiddlers that ever lived, who dug the fields, or played their music and supped their whiskey at open fires, I could not imagine a single one of them as dead.

Of all the box players who foddered cattle on rugged mountains, their coats tied with twine, or who pedalled up hills on old black Raleigh bikes, with saddles that would rupture a delicate backside, or who faced the wind on Honda

50s, I could not imagine a single one of them in the grave.

Listening to music can be like that: the clergy sleep and lack surveillance, while lovers stay forever young and all the world is woven in eternal dance, and even Yeats himself – that tattered coat upon a stick, I sensed, was tapping his foot in the wings.

After the gig the band and the crew had a few glasses of wine in the Peacock bar, and I sat in the corner with Steve Wickham talking about various ways of getting to heaven. People were squashed in on all sides of us. We talked about an old flute player in Fermanagh years ago who kept his instruments in the bath. He would go to the pub and play all day and when he came home he would play in his room, alone, till late in the night.

One day he went out to play in Swanlinbar. But in the evening he took a notion that he would like to visit an old friend, so he walked two or three miles to his house. And he knocked, but no one answered him. Then he tapped the window but there was no one at home. So he turned back for the village and realised that it was too far for him to walk, now that the fever of whiskey had worn off. So he lay down behind a wall and played a few hornpipes, scattering the notes in the wind, before heading off to heaven, on his own, and the postman found his body the following morning.

It is lunchtime and the weather is changing. May and June have been like this. The sun shines and it's warm. The sun goes in and an easterly wind cuts the nose off me.

I close the computer.

I go outside and walk across the yard towards the back

door. Inside the beloved has already returned. She has placed slices of bread on a wooden board. Cheese from the fridge. And she's at the sink rinsing salad from her garden.

I help with the sandwiches, layering the cheese and salad, and she does the more skilled operations of adding spice and various mustards.

I make the tea. We put the sandwiches on two plates and take them to the front lounge, where we can look out the window.

There's a bird box attached to an alder tree. We watch it keenly at lunchtime every day to see if anything will go in or come out. Perhaps it's too low to the ground. Perhaps it's too near the house.

So far we haven't seen a bird entering or emerging. But it's sufficient conversation. We continue to abide by that principle that there is no need for much conversation when the love is deep and the sandwiches are so tasty.

So we drink our tea and gaze out at the empty bird box and wonder silently about the world. There's no point in checking the news yet. That could unravel our serenity. It's too early in the day to allow anxiety to spill out into the room. Both of us must spend the rest of the afternoon as we did the morning. In our own solitude. In calm abiding. In our own creativity. Holding our own uncertain futures in our hearts.

When we emerge from this lockdown but find we are still masked, covered, and watched with caution by strangers, and when we are going about our business once again, just as before except for the anxiety and fear in our eyes, I will miss this moment, the music of this hour. The blackbird and the pheasant and the wind in the trees. Even the cackle of the magpies and the incessant cuckoo and the squeaking of little baby birds hidden among the branches.

What we have found in this lockdown is something ancient, sublime, akin to what monks might have found in beautiful mountain places as they chanted into the dawn. What musicians found in slow airs. We found a kind of music at midday. A

What we have found in this lockdown is something ancient, sublime, akin to what monks might have found in beautiful mountain places as they chanted into the dawn.

lunchtime concert of birdsong. We sat outside and listened. While the whole woodland made music. It was alive. And we heard it every day. That's the thing that has become strange about the lockdown: being here seems perfect.

After lunch I tidied the dishes into the dishwasher and left by the back door. The camper van stood idle in the yard and I was proud of it. I had sold a little Mercedes Vito camper and my 181 Skoda Karoq, all to buy a bigger, better camper van in the autumn of 2019 in Castlebar. It was blue-grey in colour, apart from the black windows on one side, and Renault Master was splashed in black along the other side. I sat in it all through the autumn and early winter, looking out the darkened windows and listening, knowing that the time had come to write the ending of the story. How the storyteller finds the silence, like landing a boat on an island far away.

No more songs.

I'd go up the hills and park in rugged landscape looking over various beautiful valleys and lakes.

But no more stories.

I'd drive to someone's house and go inside and drink wine with the living, or say prayers with the dead if it was a funeral house, and I'd go back out to the van and lie there in a sleeping bag wrapped in a duvet, and listen to the night around me.

Just silence. Sometimes at night in the woods the sounds were like another form of silence. The little animals mooch around with stealth. Twigs break or leaves rustle almost with a gentility that is below the capacity of the ear to track. And yet I could sense it in the darkness. Out there, they were playing.

But on the seventh of June the camper van had been sitting idle for weeks apart from the one trip each Thursday to the Gala shop. So I got in and turned on the engine. Let it rev up and waken the battery. I was digesting a sandwich. My stomach felt it had work to do. I was sitting in a stationary van with the engine running, like a child who is not allowed drive it.

How simple to drive it out onto the road, down and away – anywhere.

But no.

It's a day like every other day since the twelfth of March.

Tomorrow perhaps it will be different.

Or July. Or next year. Who knows? For the moment, all I can say is the van is here and ready to go. And the battery is still in good condition.

MacIntyre couldn't drive. Cars or

vans meant nothing to him. But he knew an enormous amount about sonnets and Irish syllabic verse, and I loved his poetry, and I treated him like a teacher, like a father and master, and over the years, whenever I sat at his table, I eased more and more into the rituals of food, the dance of good conversation where you don't speak of your own work, and how to experience the pleasure of wine rather than guzzling it simply to relieve anxiety.

He lived a long life and he picked blackberries along the ditches in the morning when he was in his eighties. And sometimes when I took off in the car to travel across two counties into the drumlins of east Cavan to visit him, it felt like the most radical thing I had ever done. And sometimes just being with him for a night at the fire seemed endless, as we worked our way down a bottle of whiskey.

I would drive home the following morning as if it was the

beginning of a new life and my head singing with phrases he had used in the shadows at the fireside.

'Walk over the cliff blindfolded,' he would urge me over and over again, 'and do it every day, without fail.'

If only he had lived in a world where Irish was as fluently spoken as Arabic in the lands of Rumi. Then he would have been heard. But forced to sing in the English language both illustrated his originality and kept it hidden, simultaneously.

Perhaps that's the same old blockage for anyone Irish who writes in English. Sometimes I think even Latin might be a better choice. Or Arabic.

I will never forget the night he first lifted a book by Rumi off his shelf in my presence and said, 'I have something for you here.'

And his hand was trembling.

There were notes written on every page. He read a few lines and then from memory began to fill the room with beautiful thoughts from the great Sufi poet.

The book was *The Glance* by Rumi, translated by Coleman Barks, and on the opening page MacIntyre had written: 'I learn, by going where I have to go.'

I had not yet learned anything about Rumi or his ecstatic verses in which his mystical love for the beloved becomes a symbol of his love for God. And both MacIntyre and I were born into an Ireland where words minted in the age of faith were meaningless. So codes were required in a secular time to mark the same territory – to find the path without the help of the usual signposts.

The book was more than a book. The many sentences he

had underlined were more than just the tracks and traces of his reflections.

It was for me a moment of intense intimacy. He was passing to me something that could not be named. Exposing me to the tenderest aspect of his own uncertainty.

'Read it,' he said, again becoming a Zen master – the one with authority. And I did. I read it many times, following fresh and deeper signposts. I read it late into the nights when I was stricken with depression, and in moments of elation, hand in hand with my own beloved, on beaches in Donegal and on the streets of Warsaw.

'Will you meet me on the inside or on the outside?' I often asked her late at night.

But I was only quoting Rumi.

'Will you meet me on the inside or on the outside,' I often whispered in the dark, on many nights when there was no one else in the room.

But of course I have always loved the night. I was in Paris twenty years ago on the occasion of the Nuit Blanche. I hadn't a clue what was going on. I wandered around the old student quarter, near Rue des Irlandais, confused at first by the lights in every shop, and the crowds on the streets, though it was after midnight.

In the lit-up city restless lovers wandered along the boulevards, and young people queued for crepes at the corner of every street.

Along the Seine big glass buildings had been transformed into television screens. The facades of a train station flickered with a giant projection of Humphrey Bogart.

Near pavement cafés the air was heavy with perfume, the aroma of coffee and cigarette smoke. There were enough lights blazing to attract E.T. back to earth. Museums were open and in various little galleries Parisians admired the art.

'All the galleries are open,' I exclaimed to a waitress in a bar near the Pantheon. 'Even Notre Dame is open. It's amazing.'

She had long hair, and huge brown eyes, and a tiny white apron around her waist.

There were photographs of Sartre and Camus on the walls. The bare floorboards and the red upholstery on the seats

There were enough lights blazing to attract E.T. back to earth.

looked like they hadn't been changed since the days when Nazi officers strutted about the Luxembourg Gardens. Ireland wasn't over-run by Nazis but in those years little Ireland was smothering beneath de Valera's musty overcoat, and it took a very long time to escape. I tried to explain to the waitress that despite centuries of repression we were also a cultured people.

I tried to explain to her that in our country we also stay up late, singing and playing music. 'Even in winter, when the wind from Fermanagh roars over the rushy beards of Cuilce

　　　　　WHAT IS BEAUTIFUL IN THE SKY

Mountain, we huddle at the kitchen range, reciting poetry and quarrelling about metaphysical issues until dawn.'

She zig-zagged between the tables with plates of food, and she served me a stew of boiled bacon and potato, which I washed down with two bottles of wine.

I couldn't keep my eyes off her, and we chatted in English whenever she passed my table.

'I saw a musician place his fiddle case on the bonnet of a Volvo one night,' I said, 'in the middle of Tubbercurry, and take out his instrument, and play a slow air, just to welcome the dawn.'

'Irish people drink too much,' she joked.

'And long ago, at Christmas time, the mountains glowed as people walked down the slopes to midnight mass with lanterns and torches in their hands.'

'What are you talking about?' she wondered.

'Nuit Blanche,' I replied. 'We don't keep all the lights on but we have our own kind of Nuit Blanche in Ireland. We make poetry in the dark. We sing songs in the dark. We play pianos and dance in the dark and make violins talk such things that would soften the heart of a prison guard.'

'You talk too much,' she said. 'You need to relax. Lighten up. Nuit Blanche is just for fun. But if you wait until I finish work, I can take you to my studio. I am an artist.'

We walked through the city, past the Pompidou Centre where a friend of hers was distributing anti-nuclear leaflets, and a boy from Clare was playing a didgeridoo.

The four of us went back to her studio. There were unfinished paintings on the floor, and white canvases leaning against the walls, and a bare bulb near the ceiling.

The Clare boy and the anti-nuclear woman went to bed – a vast mattress in the corner. A boy's paradise of black ribbon and soft lace.

I sang – 'Raglan Road' – in a cloud of patchouli, amid scented candles and the tang of linseed oil.

'Lovers should stay up all night,' I declared.

'Au contraire,' she replied. 'If we were lovers, we would go to bed.'

I was so terrified of committing the literal act of love with her that I dilly-dallied around the subject until 6 a.m., quoting poems by Neruda.

'In Ireland staying up all night is a sort of contraceptive,' I admitted. Finally.

She said, 'Paris never sleeps.' And we danced a little then, before the flat grey light of morning brought me down to earth and I bade her farewell and went home. But that was a long time ago, before I grew too old for dancing.

MacIntyre was like a mother sometimes. Not just with young women or people sick in hospital. But even with me.

He cooked me fish, and sheltered me in his house and put his arms around me. In his big soft jumpers I felt a cherishing mother embracing me.

It's what the child does at night when it's frightened and then wakes at dawn all safe and happy.

And there I was, hungover, him at the curtains letting in the sunlight. And he laughed, and said, 'Me life on you, but you're leaping out of your skin.'

He died at Samhain, in 2019, and when the funeral was over I didn't know what to do. So I wrote him a letter.

Dear Tom

I went to your house last night. I was there before, on an autumn day when you were watching Donegal play in the Ulster final, and the cat sat on the top of the sofa looking down at us, and your beloved carried soup from the kitchen and the smell wafted along the corridor.

And I was there one year later when you grew feeble, went into the woods of your own imagination, sat at the table staring at a poem, until finally you were confined to the pillow, your face fallen into the quiet repose of a pilgrim.

You were my oak tree, withering slowly, gracefully. You were my compass. My mountain river.

But last night your house was empty. I saw the casket of wicker. I saw the gaunt bones stretched in a suit. I saw the people gathered.

But the house was empty.

The poet was no more.

And then on the way home I remembered your voice, telling that old story about the trapdoor you fell through as a child.

There was a trapdoor at one end of the loft. And nothing would do me but to find it. Even if I didn't know I was searching for it. I rambled my way to it, the foxglove looking at me, the clover smelling, the daisies basking, the buttercups shiny, and the

trapdoor, somehow, not fastened.

I'm gone.
Fifteen-foot drop to the stable below.
But.

A lap of hay was waiting for me. It saved me. It wasn't supposed to be there. But it was.

And when people ask me what I believe in, I invariably say a lap of hay.

I too believe in angels, Tom, that catch us when we fall. And it was you who taught me to say my prayers to them. And it was you who taught me that the only story worth telling is a love story.

Your house is silent now. And empty.

So what could I do this morning but go tell the bees. Tell the robin. Tell the magpies and badgers, the foxglove and clover. Tell the hills and drumlins, the lakes and rivers, the hedgerows of berries. Tell them the house is empty. I did.

But the bees spoke back to me. The robin replied.

'No,' they said. 'No. The house is never empty. As long as love lacks surveillance, as long as love is sung, spoken, danced, the house is never empty.'

Love is everywhere. Behind us. Above us. Below us. Beside us. And inside and outside. Everywhere.

And so, dear Tom, I pray with confidence that somewhere beneath a Cavan sky, near the lakeshore, and in the rustle of an oak tree, you will find once again today that lap of hay. As angels lead you into paradise.

My stomach had done its duty. I had digested the sandwich. I had warmed the engine of the van. I turned off the ignition, got out and locked it, then walked back to my study. Inside it was cold. The fire had gone out.

I used another firelog and a match and four briquettes to rekindle it. I closed the door and sat listening to the lick of flames in the grate sucking oxygen. Before the lockdown I might have gone to Drumshanbo for lunch. Then perhaps a nap by the fire in the afternoon. It cost money, and diesel, and the time to travel there and back. And sometimes it seemed that such idleness was necessary to fill the day.

At least in the lockdown life is cleaner, and the air is cleaner and my mind gradually gets cleaner. There is less to distract.

We eat sandwiches now. It's simple. And we watch the bird box. And when I fall asleep or doze in the afternoon the images in dreams are stronger, more intense.

When I dream I am in Paris, I can almost smell the cigarette smoke of long ago. I can hear Tom MacIntyre's voice as if he were in the room. As if he were sitting at the stove beside me.

'Where have all the people gone?' he wonders.

'They're in lockdown,' I explained.

'What's lockdown?' he enquires.

And then I open my eyes. And my own words come back to haunt me. The room is never empty. As long as love lacks surveillance, as long as love is sung, spoken, danced, the house is never empty. Because love is everywhere. Behind us. Above us. Below us. Beside us. And inside. And outside. Everywhere. And I think it was that very afternoon. After lunch. After sitting in the van for twenty minutes. After dozing by the fire for an hour. I think it was then that I woke up completely. The words I had spoken in the church at his funeral finally floated up in my own conscious mind and they spoke themselves to me and I heard them as if they were being spoken by someone else.

I felt as if Tom were in the room speaking them to me. I felt as if all his life had been gathered up into that single intense moment. As if in the empty room he was present by his absence. And his absolute absence made him absolutely present.

What was in those sandwiches?

I texted to the beloved. With a laughing emoji. But it's amazing how simple a lunch can be. Even if I couldn't go to a restaurant in Carrick-on-Shannon, on the seventh of June 2020, because of the lockdown.

There's a drawing of a horse framed on the wall of my study. It was

made by my daughter when she was in primary school. I sit staring at it in the afternoon light. The sun has shifted across the sky, slightly more to the west. The room's south-facing patio doors can no longer catch a spill of direct sunlight. The intensity has gone out of the day.

And this is how I know the day: by the sun's position in the garden. Each shift carries a different emotional tone. In the mornings light blazes on the lawn area that slopes towards the lake. At midday it rests directly above the trees and the patio gets hot and the foliage of trees to the south becomes a shelter for me and for small birds that nest in the woodland.

In the afternoon the sun goes further west on the road, slanting back from Mayo across the top of the roof. It reaches across the lake and hits the slopes of Sliabh an Iarainn straight on, making the heather glow and little houses glisten and the bogland turn rusty in the evening light.

The daughter is in England working in a stable yard. The horse drawing on the wall has nobody to admire it but me. And all I can think of is the Ballinasloe fair. I went to it one year because my daughter's love for horses had made me curious. I felt I knew so little about her. She was a stranger to me at seven years of age. Where did she come from? I wondered. What previous life did she complete before choosing us?

I arrived in Ballinasloe at noon. The streets were jammed with hucksters, traders, and young Traveller girls in hot pants and miniskirts, adorned with earrings and bracelets – a brash parade of cultural assertion, driven by a heady mix of adolescent uncertainty, social exclusion and sexual repression. It was a cold day to be tipping through the horse manure in toe-crunching stilettos, bare-shouldered and bare-bellied.

I heard the ghost of Margaret Barry at a street corner singing 'She Moved Through the Fair', and I was so mesmerised by young women that I hardly paid attention to the horses standing idle and gentle beneath the blue sky.

I was never good with animals. Apart from loving cats, I have stood aloof from wild beasts. But there is something unbearably tender about falling in love with a horse, or shedding tears on the television because your cows have been slaughtered, or preserving a herd of sheep that was once tended by your grandfather. That was the kind of compassion that emerged during the foot-and-mouth crisis in Ireland twenty years ago. I remember being in Delvin at that time, the town where Lawrence of Arabia's ancestors once ran their hounds, and where there is an ancient monastic ruin, near to which a friend of mine dug up the cranium of a monk by accident; he thought it was a donkey's skull. In the cattle mart there was a restaurant, where men waited for breakfast.

A girl from Eastern Europe brought plates of hot food to the tables, and there was an air of excitement as farmers in old jumpers and trousers that might have been lying on the floor of some byre for centuries set aside their staffs and removed their baseball caps before tucking into a fried breakfast.

Then everyone went to the rings. In one area a lot of furry pedigree lambs were being auctioned by a man in a white coat. I toyed with the idea of a cuddly sheep at the end of my bed instead of a cat, but decided against it. In the main ring anonymous heifers stumbled into the lights, terror in their eyes as they got walloped with sticks.

Although I saw an old and frail white-haired man stretching his hand beyond the barrier and touching the flank of an agitated calf. The beast turned to face him, scrutinising the old man as he petted its trembling head and pulled its ears with delicacy.

Where that old man might be now, twenty years later, I don't know. Alive or dead. Forgotten in some nursing home. Or not. I cannot say. But that one drawing of a horse by my daughter had led me through another meandering path of memory – one memory after another, and finally to him. And then back to her, because I think of her often too, away in England.

Random ghosts become mentors for my soul. The old man reaches his hand to touch the flank of an agitated beast forever, always just beyond my fingertips, healing wounds in me that I am hardly aware of, though I can feel their pain like a fog of unease surfacing from time to time.

And you'd have to admire the virus: a tiny bug that could kill so many, a tiny microbe that could sting the world to death. There's no doubt that during the lockdown, and in self-isolation, the virus punished me. But as I found myself spending long

> And you'd have to
> admire the virus:
> a tiny bug that could kill
> so many, a tiny microbe
> that could sting
> the world to death.

hours alone in a room I began to notice a change. Not just in the sky, or the seeming abundance of wildlife, but in myself. I would not remain the same in the time of the virus. That was clear. I would not be the same when it was over. I began to feel the possibility of transformation. Though I didn't understand what I might become.

Covid-19 was trying to waken me. Opening me raw. Killing layers of me that had accrued over decades: the scales on my eyes, the crusts on my soul. Even as its venomous fangs were invisible in the wind, it offered me rebirth.

The virus had the power to drag me to itself, to make me swallow it unknowingly. It could eat my lungs, and kiss the muscles of my heart with its tiny, delicate fangs. This intimate bug. This unwelcome virus. This tender plague. It could lead or nudge or drag anybody to the grave, or if it could be avoided, then to a new beginning.

I should go to therapy more often and talk about these things. But I gave that up. Just like religion, I grew dislocated from therapy. And I have no reference points any longer for my unconscious. I just dream and drift, and let the world unfold like rippling water, and I walk in it as best I can with the guides that my imagination gives me. Moriarty. MacIntyre. John O'Donohue. Father, uncle and brother. And all the strangers and enemies that lurk below the surface of the conscious mind. And all the accidental storytellers in every hairdressing salon and every Gala cafeteria in the country – still singing out their wisdom like terns or gulls, still offering hymns of praise from the unconscious heart of Ireland, in its confusion and irrational wonder, like waves on a beach forever.

The virus deprived everyone of normal activity, and deadened motivation, and confused every well-laid plan, as the world went to sleep and deep into a tunnel of isolation. MacIntyre would have loved it.

'Loosen your grip,' he would say, 'and let go of the why. The universe unfolds at its own pace.'

Of course among the many ghosts who began to surround

me, Tom MacIntyre also called at regular intervals through the lockdown. But there was no why now.

No why to the mystery of light; or to why light moves at the speed of light and never any faster or slower. It's just a truth without causality. Like most of everything that makes up life. So stop stressing and clenching your fist, I say to myself, and stop worrying about Covid-19 or when this isolation will be over.

Maybe pray.

If that's what you need to do.

Maybe.

Shortly after MacIntyre's funeral, I posted the letter to myself. It wasn't a letter

if I didn't stamp it and send it, so I sent it to myself.

I dropped it into a letterbox outside the post office in Carrick-on-Shannon and promised myself a treat in a restaurant called The Happy Place. I would cheer myself up with a crepe.

But first I strolled around the town, as was my habit since the heart attack. Up and down Main Street, past the church, down by the river, over the bridge to Lunny's petrol station and back again, all the time giving praise to God that I was alive.

No. More truthfully, feeling grateful to be alive considering my dear friend, the immutable tower of wisdom and strength in the matter of writing, was now as dead as a dead fly. It's the first way the dead speak to us. Their going awakens our sense of life. Simply being on two feet after a funeral is liberating. It's no wonder Irish people delight in going to one funeral after another.

The streets were dry, the walk was pleasant and when I arrived at The Happy Place it was empty.

The young woman behind the counter appeared pregnant. She smiled at me in the way people smile when they see something funny. She was self-contained, on that threshold moment in life that pregnant women exude: radiant on the verge of motherhood. I heard her talking on the phone and her voice was gentle and soft.

And my own daughter was gone to Melbourne, though I didn't allow the thought to fester.

'What have you got on the menu today?' I wondered.

'Crepes,' she said. 'We always have crepes on the menu. What kind do you want?'

I didn't know.

'We do a simple crepe with lemon and ice-cream,' she said. 'Would you like that?'

Where will I sit? I asked myself, and I went to a corner near the window, and she began to spread the creamy batter on the crepe pan.

The place was warm and cosy so I took off my coat and draped it over the next chair, placed my peaked cap on the seat, made some re-arrangements to my gaudy red tie and the tweed waistcoat that covered my bulging stomach. There are good restaurants and great ones. For me the good ones are warm and cosy, but the great ones are like country kitchens. Places where the staff operate as if they were nourishing their uncles, grandmothers and sisters. Places where the staff have time to chat to each other, and where serving the customers becomes mere punctuation in the protracted conversations they conduct behind the counter regarding what the dentist said yesterday about their child's tooth, or why their mother won't go to Aldi as a matter of principle.

These are the places I used to sit and open my ears and let in all the stories and small wonders that pepper the lives of ordinary people – the narratives that marked a wider truth of life beyond my own small ego.

These are the places I used to sit and open my ears and let in all the stories and small wonders that pepper the lives of ordinary people

The restaurants I went to in Carrick-on-Shannon were quiet and safe spaces. There were more than buns and crepes and half dinners and latte coffees on offer. There was a faint nostalgia in the air. A sense of a long-ago kitchen where Mammy was eternally sitting over the range steaming cabbage in a single pot with the bacon.

I think Lunny's garage offered the best latte. It had half a dozen tables in a dedicated corner, and a counter dedicated to serving coffees and teas by young women who probably came from Poland or Lithuania. I asked one day for an extra-hot latte and it came in a mug that I could hardly touch without burning my fingers.

I returned a week later and looked her in the eye and before I could open my mouth she said, 'A latte, extra hot?'

She had won me.

Esquires was another place I enjoyed, particularly for the excellent pots of tea. It was fancy in the sense that the affluent young women of Leitrim would lounge near a big glass window, with shopping bags at their feet, and talk about weddings they were at in Kilronan Castle. Young men in business suits sometimes met sales reps coming from Dublin, since it was on the edge of town as traffic came in from the east.

And Giovanni's was of course my favourite for real chips: fresh and hand-cut, and served with fried eggs and beans. It was run by Romanians. But when I looked in over the steel-rimmed counter and saw them shaking the chips in the oil, or flattening pizza bread for the oven, they always reminded me of Donegal. I don't know why.

There were other magical places, like the back lounge in the Bush Hotel, where I could never resist a carvery dinner, and Lena's Tea Room, a magical space of vintage chairs and tables and old-fashioned pots of hot tea where I could never resist bringing intimate friends because it had an air of antiquity and reserve and I always felt I could sit on one of the sofas all day over a pot of tea and nobody would bother me.

I hope those places will all be there when the lockdown is over and that we can begin again. Although at the height of the virus I was beginning to fear that the world as we knew it was gone forever.

Restaurants where old men could find a corner, and a place to belong, eating their daily meal and feeling part of a community – just on the edge of the light, or a little distance from the heat.

Greasy spoons in London and New York, and Asian street shops across the world provided mighty refuge for the hungry, and coffee houses in Warsaw and Paris had as much space as was once available in churches for solitary pilgrims who wanted to stare out the window for hours. The kitchen zones of shopping malls all held and cherished that marginal cluster of isolated men and women in cheap trainers clutching backpacks with nothing inside them, whose eyes glazed like wounded animals as they searched for comfort.

But there was nothing quite like the joy of an Irish diner; cafeterias and dining areas in various malls, streets, or petrol stations around the country, where just sitting down in a corner was like turning up at a family gathering.

I suppose nothing is permanent and things have always been changing. We need to accept that what's gone is gone, and hope that with social distancing and sanitisers and protective glass at the counters the world will begin to spin once more.

I was singing the praises of such places to an old Italian man, early one midsummer morning in the fruit market in Dublin in 2009.

'Can we go for coffee somewhere nice?' I asked him.

'Sure,' he said, 'but you won't find joy anywhere here.'

Fyffes' loading bay, in the Dublin Fruit Market near Smithfield, was a mundane world of trucks, and men in hard hats and yellow jackets whizzing around on forklifts, carrying produce to the lorries.

One old merchant showed me where the fish market used to be.

'I was here the morning they demolished it,' he said, pointing at a car park. 'There was even an air-raid shelter in that corner, and it took the demolition squad ages to smash it. It makes me cry to think of what they destroyed.'

We were both helpers on Fergal Fox's lorry, loading pallets of fresh fruit for his shop in Mullingar.

'Maybe you come down to Smithfield,' the Italian said. 'I show you good place when we have loaded the truck.'

When the work was done he guided Fergal to park on the kerb beside a small coffee shop serving breakfasts near Green Street.

We parked on the double yellow lines, went into the restaurant and bought breakfast rolls and coffees and ate outside, standing near enough to the lorry so we could see any traffic wardens that might be irritated by it. It was early June.

'Midsummer is always romantic time,' the Italian said. 'I'm thirty years married, and each year I bring my wife for dinner.'

His teeth sank into a bilberry muffin, and then he intoned the names of various restaurants.

'The Monaco. The Cafolla. Fortes. The Green Rooster. The Broadway. All of them, beautiful restaurants.'

He finished his bun and wiped crumbs from his lips.

'The Mayfair. The Lido. The Maple Leaf. And the one in Abbey Street – what was it called? – The Ritz? Yes. I took the wife to them all. Hey! Is there anything better?'

He looked wistfully into the blue sky. But he wasn't finished.

'Bernardo's. Le Caprice. Fantastic food.'

He spoke the names like prayers. As if he were invoking Italy around us, and when we left him he was almost in tears. Because nothing is permanent.

'That's two sad men I met this morning,' Fergal Fox declared. 'First you. Then him. I bet I'll meet a third before nightfall. 'Cos things always come in threes.'

But I understand his sadness now. He missed Italy. For thirty years in Dublin he still missed his homeland. And he lived out his days walking streets where ghosts looked out at him from cafés and restaurants that had changed so much he hardly recognised them. Or else they were not there anymore. It occurred to me that my own life might be the same as I drive across the country in the future, pointing at derelict buildings along the way, on the outskirts of various towns, saying, 'Look. That's where I used to have my soup or cups of coffee.'

And Fergal Fox was right. That evening there was a barbecue: burgers on the lawn beneath the beech trees outside Mullingar, while the neighbours sipped wine on the patio, and young people made a bonfire from wood they wheel-barrowed out of a farmer's shed – though the farmer wasn't amused. Then everyone circled the blazing bonfire and the music began and people held and hugged each other, and kissed each other with abandon.

A woman brought her bodhrán and a bag of whistles. Each time the guitar man changed key she'd reach into her bag for another whistle, like a mechanic poking for a different wrench.

She told me her grandfather was the first bodhrán player with The Chieftains. One freezing November evening in the early sixties Paddy Moloney drove down to Westmeath to meet him. But the man's wife hated the bodhrán with a passion and banned it from the house. She said he was only a fool to be playing an old drum. So he used to hide the instrument in the rafters of the barn.

When Moloney arrived, the old man had to sneak out,

unbeknownst to his wife, collect the bodhrán from the shed and go to a neighbour's house to play it.

We were all laughing at this when the fiddle player arrived. A gentle giant from a distant parish, who takes his emotional burdens out of bed each morning and carries them around all day, like dead fish. A quiet man who reeks of sorrow, and who, according to those that knew, could sigh as loud as a donkey brays.

> # A gentle giant from a distant parish, who takes his emotional burdens out of bed each morning and carries them around all day, like dead fish.

He grew up in a cottage, but when his father died he built a bungalow along the roadside, 'so the mother would be nearer the church'. But they say that for years afterwards he'd often go up to the derelict cottage and just sit in the kitchen and stare at the wall.

For a while he sat on the patio, listening to other guests with mighty attention. He was like a haystack, absorbing any amount of emotion they threw at him, and no matter how much sniping or whinging went on around him, he just listened and nodded, and looked at the ground.

That's when Fergal Fox came over and nudged me. 'There's another sad man. I knew we'd find the third.'

But appearances can be deceptive, because when eventually he took the bow to his fiddle, the music that rose up was so fierce I thought the fairies must have arrived for Midsummer, and that they were dancing wildly inside him.

Such barbecues are also a kind of restaurant, an eating trough where everyone is welcome – including old men clinging to their fiddles or flutes, waiting their turn to be asked into the limelight.

MacIntyre took me to the best restaurants in Dublin and he would take the bill and make so little of it that I came to expect it. I ate his food like he was a mother. And if I mentioned it he would say that he wouldn't have survived when he was my age were it not for the elders who helped him.

'This is Ireland,' he would say. 'We mind each other.'

Although he did mention one famous writer who had a fine job in the university but was not mindful of any pauperised poet.

'I was in extremis at one point when I was living on Inisbofin, fishing pollock for lunch and shooting rabbits for dinner,' he joked. 'So I sent him what I thought was an eloquent letter stating my case but I never heard from him. Some years later I met him at a book launch and enquired whether he ever got the note. He said not. And then, when I returned to the island a week later, I found an envelope on the doorstep with a pound note neatly folded within.'

It was around that time that I met MacIntyre, when he had abandoned his island life and was en route to Paris to find work in theatre, and I was into my third year as a young teacher in west Cavan. Leaving the island had been an enormous emotional upheaval for him, and as he said himself, standing at the top of the stairs in a priest's house, it was fortuitous that I had walked in the door.

The house was the curate's castle in Doobally near Dowra in county Cavan. The priest, his brother, was away on holidays. MacIntyre was alone. The door was open and I heard a cry from upstairs.

'Help.'

I saw him standing on the landing in a dressing gown. Like he might have a fever.

'Thank God you're here,' he said, clutching the banister, as if he could tumble down any moment. And then he staggered back towards the bedroom door and fell onto the bed.

I went up to the landing and gazed at him, now propped up with pillows. I wondered if he might need a doctor, a priest, his brother, a psychotherapist, or another writer.

'I just need fish,' he said. And he insisted I go to the kitchen, find a fish in the fridge, perhaps one he had taken with him from the island, and cook it. I did so, brought it to the bed, and he ate it in silence.

Who is this white-haired man? I wondered. And what am I doing here? But I had no explanation as to why I was behaving as if he were my master.

'And now,' he declared, his eyes turning the colour of sea waves in bright sunlight, 'I may need some rum, for medical reasons.'

I drove to Dowra, six miles away, bought bottles of rum and blackcurrant juice and we began a five-day session of discovery.

'Will you return tomorrow evening?' he asked me, before I left.

'I don't even know why I'm here tonight,' I replied.

'You're a writer, are you not?' he declared. 'That's why you're here. There are no accidents in life.'

> I drove to Dowra,
> six miles away, for bottles
> of rum and blackcurrant
> juice and we began
> a five-day session
> of discovery.

After that I came to him each evening directly after my teaching day ended at four o'clock and we talked until night in riddles, and songs, and meaningless conundrums. We heard the curlew dreaming, and the blackbird dreaming, and we watched the mountain fading into silhouette as twilight seeped up from the bogland, and we saw the moon rising over Éadan Mór and spill a pallid light in through the window and dance upon the bare floorboards with such grace that it silenced both of us.

I felt as if I had found a father, a guide to the realm of wonder. For he never spoke of the mundane, and the relationship was never as ordinary as a friendship. He was my senior, my mentor, and I was his student. Other than that we had no dependency on each other and nothing emotional complicated the ferocity of that learning.

Yet for over forty years we met regularly and invoked the gods, the great mothers, the poets of long ago and the spirits of the woodland, and we recovered each time a transcendent light that once the moon had dropped in the window of a priest's house in Doobally in 1975.

And as the dusk settled and resettled around us evening after evening in the years ahead, and as we sat by various blazing fires, I always rejoiced in that accidental moment when I went through his door.

Not that it was easy to sit with MacIntyre. Like an ancient philosopher, he interrogated his company with disturbing variations of a single question.

'What are you doing with your life?'

And he could sit for hours without speaking. Just sifting the silence, staring at the flames so that all I could see in the shadows were his sparkling eyes. He watched the fire like a fisherman waiting for a salmon to hop out of an estuary.

Almost at the end of his life, I saw him attend a festival in his honour conducted in the town of Bailieboro where he had been born eighty years earlier. The climax of the weekend was a poetry reading in the courthouse – a lofty room of shadow and dust with dark wooden benches for lawyers and a great podium with a backdrop of red velvet curtains where the imperial judges once presided over the cantankerous disputations of the district.

The courtroom was a good choice for the poetry reading because writers were seen as outlaws for centuries in the drumlin landscape of south Ulster – a class of anarchists in the Gaelic mode that were beyond the surveillance of state or church, or the forces of the crown.

For centuries the ordinary people of rural Ireland saw poets almost like an alternative priesthood. Poets spoke out of the unconscious. They were shamans and mediums of the soul's invisible light. They were witnesses to the holy door, the portal of sacred things. They used words to get beyond words. They opened the doors that the church invariably kept locked. They were standard-bearers for the invisible realm that neither judge nor cleric nor officer of the crown could ever control.

That was the tradition that MacIntyre was born into, and eighty years later he rose to speak, an elderly man with white hair, and a soft but intense voice that contained the thunder of a life lived intensely and the controlled inflections of an experienced lover and performer. He stood for a moment in silence until he had gained attention. A pin dropping would have been noted.

'I remember being a child,' he began, 'and dreaming of two horses: a brown and a dove grey. It was my first dream, and now recently I see them again. They return in old age. Though not so much the brown, but more frequently the dove grey.'

In the modern world this might have sounded obscure. Even at some poetry festival in the city I could imagine people reaching for multiple references and instantly expecting a dissertation on psychoanalysis.

But on the rugged faces of the unlettered people that packed into the courtroom in Bailieboro, who knew him since he was a child, and knew his mother and who saw him grow, bone of their bones, with nothing before him but the grave, his meaning was different.

His meaning had no meaning. The dream was to be relished, not explained. His poetry was full, complete in itself, and always tragically funny, in a way that poetry rarely is in modern society – not because poetry had failed but because society had long ago failed to feel poetry on the flesh, or to speak it from the gut. Poetry for decades in English-speaking cultures had been dying from the virus of irony, that imposes on poetry a kind of deadening meaning.

But his audience opened their hearts, and on their blistered faces there was a noticeable ease as they relaxed. Because they knew he was playing. They were at home in the game of poetry.

Here was a poet who had traipsed the world from New York to Moscow with plays and poems. *The Great Hunger* had been a ground-breaking play in Irish theatre. *Rise Up Lovely Sweeney* was a unique meditation on the allure of violence that overrides even the erotic impulse in the Irish psyche.

But most of all his love songs and his translations of old love songs endures. His attachment to all the haunted lakes in Cavan, his relish for words and all their juicy innuendos marked him out as an unruly bard in the tradition of south Ulster poets that reaches back to people like Cathal Buí Mac Giolla Ghunna, Peadar Ó Doirnín and Séamas Dall Mac Cuarta.

His reading in Bailieboro on that Saturday night at eighty years of age was peppered with references to ghosts and other invisible things, and the shadows in the creaking room wrapped themselves around him and gave substance to the insubstantial.

He had one big secret, though he never spoke it to me directly because its essence would have withered on his tongue: ideas cannot contain truth. They can show it, point to it and illustrate it in various ways, but they can never hold it, like the eyes hold the moon on a good night. And that was a good night in Bailieboro. And after an hour the poet rested and I could see in the eyes of his audience a clear, open expression of love. And love is a kind of knowing.

But now what time is it, I wonder?

I don't know. Because there's a portion of every afternoon that can only be described as The Big Dozing Time. It may still be a few minutes past two. The clocks may have stopped and time may have stood still. Or on the other hand it could be 3.30 p.m.

After dozing I never know, unless I measure time by the fire. And the fire is blazing, so it can't be that long a while that I have been dreaming again of MacIntyre. But I sit up suddenly and close the draught on the stove. Then I open a window because the sun has come out and by its position I may have slept an hour – and an hour too long because of the lunch in my belly.

Looking out I see the bird box. I watch it for a while. But nothing stirs. I look at the grass that I inspected this morning and I know it's still calling to me. The lawnmower awaits my arrival in the shed. The day is half gone. It's time to get the mowing over with.

But that pleases me because it's something that shapes the afternoon. It gives me a structure to the shapeless days of lockdown. It allows me out of my room. I become a worker for an hour. And as I follow the Honda machine around the slopes and curves of the garden, I get time with every tree, every shrub and wild flower. It's as if I am not a writer in the garden cutting grass. I forget everything except the trees, the bluebells and the wild garlic.

Now the lawn is done. That's definite.

Cleanly cut, cropped back to the root. The moss that was there in the first cutting of early April has all but vanished, or died off. The grass is stronger. And it's easier to cut because of that. So I put the machine in the green shed, lock it up and leave the key with the yellow label back in the kitchen on its hook, in case the beloved needs to fetch something in the shed later for her work. She usually works all day and then in the evening I find her in the vegetable patch she cultivates at the southern end of the garden beside her studio which is hidden from view behind all the trees. Or else I hear the spade.

I return to my studio to check the fire. The clock says 4.30 p.m. and the fire is almost out. I put on another two briquettes and sit. It's a good time to rest, to feel the ending of things, the completion of things. I'd have a shower and lie on the bed in the house if it were not for the fact that we have no water. We rely on a tank which collects rainwater from the roof and during the lockdown there has been no rain. So here we are, deteriorating inside our socks. The water went down each day as the lockdown continued. We have worked our way through an entire tank, just waiting.

It will be over soon; but for today we are still here. Still without water. And I have got used to life without showers. It's not a big issue. For now I am rekindling the fire in the stove and I am taking another break from reading.

My mind is often empty now.

After MacIntyre died I had no metaphors, images, poems or stories. I had no hope. Like John O'Donohue, John Moriarty and many others I have had the privilege to know, MacIntyre was wiser and more erudite than me. Like my Tibetan teacher, and like my beloved, he had gifts beyond my ken. I suppose that is what a teacher is. And a disciple, strictly speaking, is one who follows. I suppose there is some serenity in the humility that comes with age and I had followed him, like a son follows a father.

When my father died I took the loan of his Morris Minor and drove to Clare and camped on the Cliffs of Moher, and met a German woman called Beate, and after a few nights we went further south to the Puck Fair, and slept together, not knowing each other's second names and yet our souls for that one wild and windy week were as one.

I didn't ask what she had lost. I didn't need to tell her I had lost my father. I was there not just because my father had loved Clare and even brought a rose bush with him to Cavan which blossomed a pale pink every summer when I was a child. And when Beate and me got to Killorglin for the Puck Fair, and set up camp in a field, I stayed awake all night listening to the branch of a chestnut tree kiss the canvas of the tent and I felt my father's soul was pulsating in the air just beyond my fingertips.

When MacIntyre died it didn't break me like that. My beloved has my heart and nothing can be added or subtracted from that but I had lost a teacher, which is like losing a compass, and there is nothing to be said or written or sung when that relationship is broken.

In MacIntyre's death
I saw poetry die inside me.
For a month after he died
I searched to find it again.

But what a mighty dying was there, I thought. Even the ending was like another poem. I kept thinking back on his beloved wife during the service speaking those words about his last hours. 'I'm falling into some tricky spaces,' he'd said to her. And I recall my own last visit. When he had said to me that he was attending to his prayers.

We fade. It ends. The ghosts and haunted lakes, the spirits of the trees, the books and poems and all the elegant love letters are blurred as the waking mind dissolves and fades forever.

In MacIntyre's death I saw poetry die inside me. For a month after he died I searched to find it again. I hoped to be surprised at a street corner by another story some day. But the day didn't come. I hoped to wake some morning with relish for a new poem. But the poems didn't come. I looked at the sky like a child and wondered what was beautiful in it. But I had no answer. I looked at the mountains and at the birds above the house in the spruce trees and wondered what, there, could be described as beautiful? And I had no answer.

Eventually I retreated to the couch and turned on Netflix and allowed the deadening habit of news and vacuous movies fill the void where love and poetry ought to have been making narratives till the dawn. Then I would go into Carrick-on-Shannon in the camper van and walk around the town, looking for something.

I wandered through the coffee places I loved, and where I loved to write, and where at every table I had the urge as I often did in the past to phone him or send a photograph. But he was no more. And sometimes I even squinted my eyes and looked at the crowds milling about in the hope that I could see him among them, jaunting along with a big jackaroo hat over his eyes and a knitted shoulder bag on his arm. And I looked for him in men's sheds too. Or rather I listened for him in the conversations of old warriors who sat exhausted at their little stoves, in various community centres around the country.

By the time his month's mind had come, the shops were full of Christmas things and it was as if he had never lived.

A month's mind is usually marked by a service or a mass

that takes place a month after the person has been buried. It is a turning point for the mourners. The intensity of their self-isolation is ended. They discard any black mourning clothes they had been wearing. It begins a second stage of mourning, less intense, as the relatives move towards recovery over the period of the coming year. The month's mind marks a certain distance from the dead. They become accustomed to their new status, and they begin to think of the dead as saintly, perfect, and at one with all the holy ancestors that dwell in the land beyond this reality.

MacIntyre's memorial took the form of a concert in the Ramor Theatre in Virginia, packed to the doors with local people and old friends from the arts world and the theatre. It was great craic. Tommy Tiernan went on stage, and Patrick Mason, Bríd Ní Neachtain, Derbhle Crotty, Brendan Flynn and many others. Each performer took the microphone in turn to sing the praises of the poet, or remember particular moments in their lives when he mattered to them. Behind where they all sat around on the stage, there was a portrait of the poet projected on a screen. It showed him white-headed and in white clothes. The pencil lines of the drawing were as delicate as the lines of fences in the snow. More and more I thought of Rumi, and how MacIntyre's book had fallen off the shelf on the evening he died. But by the time the virus arrived in March, MacIntyre's life seemed like it had happened thousands of years ago. I had almost forgotten him. Because I had other worries. The shock of realising how precious it had been for all those years, to touch and kiss, to hug and shake hands and chat randomly in every accidental nook and cranny of the world with strangers who had no fear of me. And to discover that such a world was gone forever. If I did make an observation about MacIntyre occasionally it would have only been to say how fortunate he was to have left before the party soured. Like Leonard Cohen, who took his farewells before Trump came to power, perhaps MacIntyre too knew he was leaving before it got darker.

I have had a weakness for wise old men, or at least for that template.

Whether it was MacIntyre or some other old man I may meet tomorrow, my soul is always ready to believe and trust him as a living icon. I don't know whether or not this has something to do with the male psyche. Perhaps there is an old man in every young man, an archetype, or mythic figure, or just a ghost, who sits far down in the back of the cave hoping to be heard.

A young man has two choices. To live fully in his passions or to live as if in a dream world, where he can converse with shadows. For me my precious teachers, MacIntyre and the random collection of rogues and old chancers I have met in the many hospital waiting halls and cafeterias of the nation, have all blended into one model: they are my guides.

My teacher used to tell me that the mind should be like a lake but not a river. It should be deep but not turbulent. And it should be as clear and bright as the sky in Mongolia, where things sparkle and where in the empty blue there are always beautiful things to be seen. It should never be like the sky in Leitrim where it is always full of clouds and dark wind, and where it is easy to be negative about everything.

'The mind is like the sky,' my teacher would say, 'and your actions should be like eagles that hover very high over the world. The eagle only occasionally flaps its wings to retain height, and your actions should never be like the sparrow that does a lot of flapping but never achieves altitude.'

All through the afternoon the room had been very cosy as I rested sporadically from my last reading of the book. The stove was red hot, and dozing was a constant threat. BBC Radio 3 murmured in the distance, Yo-Yo Ma's cello notes wafting from the long soundbar on the window and the woofer on my bureau adding a tremendous mellow vibration to the lower strings.

The phone rang at about 5 p.m.

I knew it was five because the time came up first on the screen. Then the green icon saying there was an incoming call and then the General's name.

'Hello,' I said, instantly, expecting his voice on the other end of the line to reply. But it was a woman who spoke.

'This is me,' she said, 'is that you?'

'Yes,' I replied, 'this is me.'

I knew the voice. It was a staff member who looked after the General in the nursing home. She kept everyone up to date and went out of her way to be a link between him and his family.

'Yes, it's me,' I repeated. 'But what's up?'

'They did some tests on him today. He's not in good form.'

'I know,' I said. 'He rang me this morning. At cock-crow. He sounded a bit distressed. How long before you have results?'

'I don't know,' she said. 'But I'm afraid we can only hope for the best. I thought you'd like to know.'

I thanked her and I didn't ask for any further details because I didn't want to speculate. After all, I'm only a friend. I'm not part of his family. And I knew the General was old enough for Covid-19 to be a fatal sentence, if indeed he had it.

I admit that as a young man I held too rigidly to the idea of Christianity,

but over the years my teacher has helped me realise that a boat is for crossing a river – you don't walk around with it on your head – so I am lighter about religion nowadays. It is only a boat, though I still love the icons and the rituals that mark out the year, from end to end.

In November I always remember loved ones that are long gone, and friends at whose deathbeds I once kept vigil, watching them breathe their last bubble of air, as their sunken eyes looked back at me from the pillow. Tom MacIntyre the poet chose the last days of November, the time of Samhain, the Celtic festival of winter and darkness, to leave the world. It seemed in keeping with his relish for invisible realms and the more ghostly rooms of the imagination.

But the General was a different kettle of fish. A man who might have gladly fallen into the arms of such a rugged saintly patriarch as Colmcille, the aristocratic hot-headed and all-powerful abbot of a vast monastic estate.

I kept thinking that the following day, the eighth of June, would be the eve of that saint's feast. How appropriate, I thought, if the General were to pass away tomorrow or the following day.

But then I woke myself from the dream and saw with horror how odd and morbid I had turned, expecting the worst, when in fact I had no evidence at all that the General's life was in any danger. Such is the shadow that this virus has cast over us, that we begin to expect bad news at every moment.

People say things like, 'He won't last until tomorrow,' or 'She's on the way out,' whenever a hospital sends a message. As if their life was a flickering candle.

And the truth is that it's not easy to die. It takes people a long time. And sometimes when the family are first alerted and go into a panic they don't realise that days or weeks later they might still be in the same situation, poised at the bedside waiting for the last breath. It was always hard enough at the bedside in that waiting time, before death closed a lover's eyes, but now in this cloud of coronavirus it is unbearable.

Knowing that all the stories and love songs of a lifetime will be taken in a body bag to the graveyard without the full pomp of a warm Irish funeral. A lonely coffin, before the altar, without ritual or ceremony apart from perhaps a single minister with a pot of holy water. No throng of mourners crushing towards the front pews to shake the mourners' hands and no heaving in the graveyard under a hundred umbrellas. Not even rain in these dry months, that might fall on a coffin like tender kisses from heaven itself as the remains are folded back into the earth.

I finished writing the book a few days ago.

But even as six o'clock approaches today, the seventh of June, I still haven't got an ending. I'm here all day alone, apart from ninety minutes cutting the grass. And yet I haven't quite put closure on the story.

Each hour I get distracted by something else. The General. The grass. The fire almost going out.

Even MacIntyre distracts me. He's like a ghost in the room, constantly drawing my mind down long, meandering avenues of memory.

And here he comes again now, with another anecdote from history: about the day he had an encounter with an older, even more ancient, writer.

The time was the 1970s. MacIntyre was in his early forties. The senior writer was well beyond eighty. They met on Grafton Street and laughed because they had not seen each other in years.

'Tom,' the old man exclaimed, 'who will accompany me into the shadows?'

He wasn't looking for information. It was a case of the teacher asking his student and hoping for the correct answer.

'No one,' Tom replied, and they laughed again.

'Correct.'

MacIntyre told me the story over a casual drink in Ranelagh when he was still in his sixties. He still laughed. And the memory remained in my mind only as slightly as the mythic pea in the mattress until it too became a crucial turning point in my own story. A casual phrase became the precious key to my survival during the lockdown.

There is nobody to accompany any of us on the road home.

Writing an ending is something I must do for myself.

Face the room alone every day and not be afraid.

Every morning. And every evening. Praying like a Christian or like a Buddhist monk. Or not praying at all.

But alone. That's how it ends.

I watched the lovely moon when I was a child, walking beside my mother, out country roads, to a farm that used to have red-feathered chickens. I didn't even have to look up just to know what was beautiful in the sky back then.

We went for eggs and often returned in the dark. Sometimes the moon was so bright on the road that I could see my shadow casting its shape on the bushes, puddles and high stone walls on our return, and I belonged to mother and the moon. Even now in Leitrim, the moon has reigned in glory during these past few nights and it fits in well with mountains and lakes, lighting up the bogland and riverbanks or wherever I walk.

I remember kneeling in a church at a removal one night as the moon sneaked in a gothic window behind the altar and added a delicate and pallid light to the tin whistle that rested on top of a young boy's coffin.

And then there was the moon in France, down south, in the Alps, which I watched after drinking in a bar at the top of Mont Cenis with the truck driver, and the philosopher from Clare, John O'Donohue.

The three of us saw it rising over the white, snowy peaks and I have a memory of the driver crying, because he couldn't bear to live with the woman he married. He was drinking too much, and spending too much time on the road, and his marriage was falling apart. And yet because he was an alcoholic he could only observe it, unable to do anything about it.

John and I were only a few weeks ordained, and we sat either side of him in the cabin of the truck, without knowing what to do. He made his strange confession to a pair of newly ordained priests, weeping his heart out, admitting his alcoholism and the neglect of his family, and then we all sat in silence until John said the moon was beautiful.

The truck driver died first, some years later, on the streets of an English city, and John O'Donohue was taken from the world too early, plucked away at the height of his powers as a philosopher. And sometimes when I see the full moon I feel a shiver of unease in his absence. The moon has always had the power to open human hearts, and reach its light into our memories, and make us sad.

One November night in Mullingar it shone through the window of a nineteenth-century farmhouse in Shandonagh where I lived. We were having dinner when the roof of the shed was suddenly drenched in silver light. The guests observed it through a lattice window and were stirred with romantic emotions. A woman leaned over to me during the coffee and said, 'I heard that you love Emmylou Harris.'

I confessed that I did, and she began singing one of Emmylou's love songs, her face so close to mine that I could feel her breath on my eyelashes. I listened, and noticed the moonlight on the white, frosty corrugated roof of the shed, and it was as if we were in the Alps again, and I was glad to be alive.

A woman leaned over to me during the coffee and said, 'I heard that you love Emmylou Harris.'

In Fermanagh they used to tell a story about a fellow who travelled to the ends of the earth. Eventually he came up against a wall made of blue cloth – but it was the sky. And he cut a small hole with his knife, and thrust his head through, just to see what was on the other side. When he returned home he told everyone what he had seen.

'Fuck all,' he said. 'Not much there at all. Just a pile of old moons heaped up in the corner.'

The meaning of it: the moon is behind everything, a

lantern under the skin, an abundance of moons on the other side of the blue.

I get sad when the moonlight makes a stencil of the trees around me, but when it touches my face, and kisses my lips, then I am at home. And no matter where I am, it is the same moon.

The poet Dermot Healy once wrote a beautiful poem in which he declared that 'the moon above Sligo is not the moon above Mayo'.

And he was right.

But the opposite is also true: the moon above Lough Allen is the same moon that shines above Beijing.

I was standing in the foyer of a Dublin hotel one night and the place was jammed with backpackers waiting to check in. I stood behind a girl from China. Her feet were in small leather slippers, and behind black hair her ears were adorned with silver rings. She was alone, distressed, and far from home. Nor could she speak much English. And the night porter was grumpy and wanted her passport and she could not understand him.

'I am foreigner,' she confessed to him with shame. 'I not understand you.'

But to me she was not foreign. To some man far away she was a precious daughter. I imagined him waving farewell, as she stepped out in her shoes to travel to the ends of the earth. And if she had a father who worked late in Beijing and if he looked up at the full moon, perhaps he would have seen what I saw. Time comes and moons come, and eventually you don't need anyone to point you towards it. It is the same moon everywhere. You know exactly where. And you know it's always there even when it's not.

The Light of the Moon

In 1969 I was a teenager on a summer course learning Irish in Donegal;

billeted in a little cottage of shadows. At midnight I slipped out a bedroom window while the other students were sleeping. The bean a' tí had long gone with her husband to their room at the rear of the house, where they snored in harmony, like two boats moored together.

I walked the un-tarred road that meandered like a ribbon into the bog and towards a lake. I was bursting with not just an unfocused love for all the girls in the summer school in their summer skirts and blouses but a love that made every blade of boggy grass and fern and heather a sensual delight, and in the dark the faint tang of turf smoke lasted in the air like perfume. I was wondering what beautiful thing I might see or hear if I continued further out there into the dark. Perhaps I wanted God to hold me together as I waited for my Intermediate Certificate results, or perhaps I just needed a kiss.

After walking past the lake and coming eventually to the shore, I heard a fisherman in his boat, lamping in the estuary – a grown man grunting and splashing in the silky black water. I remember the sound of his oars, sloshing in and out of the tide, and the wood creaking beneath the oar locks as he landed. He was no more than a shadow in the distance, but later I saw him burning sticks, and boiling a kettle on his fire, and sitting there humming to himself, some song I did not recognise.

And I loved him like no other. I loved his authority and masculinity, and his solitude and quietude, and especially the fact that he seemed to blend into the shadows of night and the inky ocean. He was at one with the entire universe.

For a moment he was God. And he came back again and again in my life in the form of various teachers and lovers and beloved companions. But he was the original one. And I will never forget him.

When the sun rose the next morning I walked towards the schoolhouse, whistling so loudly that my fellow students wondered what was wrong with me. There was no point in telling them that I had ventured out at midnight and found such a mysterious presence. A presence so old it made me feel young, so close to air that it made my flesh feel more alive. A father so singular in his masculinity that it made me feel like a girl.

Maybe that's why Donegal became the end of the story. And by the time Easter came around in 2020 everything was in place and Donegal had become the completion of the story.

For many the ocean is full of ghosts: dead fishermen, and loved

ones lost at sea. But it also hums with life – seals and dolphins and things that swim in the dark.

For me it's the most comforting of places. When I stand on the shoreline I feel that some remote presence in the depth of it is watching me.

The shoreline is also a place people go when they want to mark significant moments. A place to say things like: 'I love you.' 'It's over.' or 'I am not well.'

And I've always noticed that people who live beside the ocean make a lot of music, though they talk less than folk who live in the midlands. I suppose the ocean's hum makes human discourse superfluous.

At the shoreline there is a vast 'elsewhere'. It's above my head. It creeps up to my bare feet. It touches me with a presence so strong that I fall naturally into a state of attention and calm abiding.

The world is different at the seaside, or at the edge of an ocean. There's a sense of permanence. A sense of some presence beyond us, which goes on for longer, and from which we came and to which we will some day return.

And so one autumn morning a few weeks after the poet's funeral I was with the beloved in a Donegal hotel sucking a slice of lemon that came with the darne of salmon for breakfast. I was staring out at the ocean. My daughter was on the other side of the world, creating her own narrative, and the sweep of the white waves crashing against the black rocks appeared familiar. There was nothing at all significant about the morning. And yet the sea and the rocks appeared familiar. As if I had been calling myself home for years.

'Do you remember the house we stayed in seven years ago?' I asked the beloved. It was an old-fashioned house in Ranafast and had been up for renting that summer in 2013.

She remembered it well. We had been driving on the road between Gweedore and Dungloe in July of that year, and the sky was so blue we'd stopped at a filling station for diesel and I'd said to a man behind the counter that I'd love to find somewhere to holiday for a few days.

'Actually I have a cousin,' he'd said, 'who might rent you a house.'

When I'd returned to the car I was holding a piece of paper with a phone number and she'd asked me what was wrong.

'What would you say to a week up here by the sea?' I'd wondered, because we had been on the road home after a reading I had done the night before at the Errigal Festival.

It was one of those spontaneous things that surfaces sometimes without any plan or forethought.

That afternoon the beloved and I had stood on the sand dunes where the grass cut our toes and the sea holly was silvery-green and we had chatted with a volunteer in a high-vis jacket who was helping direct traffic in a car park behind the sand dunes, and we had spoken to a woman whose

We had enquired about people I once knew in the locality and we were told what is always told – that 'the old ones are all dead and gone, the young ones turning grey'.

husband was once in a band with the man in the high-vis jacket. We had inquired about people I once knew in the locality and we were told what is always told – that 'the old ones are all dead and gone, the young ones turning grey'.

And then we had headed for Ranafast.

The woman who was renting the house had been waiting. We spoke in Irish. I told her that I had once spent a summer at the Irish college, and I mentioned my bean a' tí's name, and that I still remembered her with affection.

'It's a small world,' the woman had observed.

'Why?' I'd wondered.

'Your bean a' tí was my aunt,' she'd said. 'The house you're about to rent is where she came from.'

We had found the house by accident but sometimes it's hard to resist magical thinking. The possibility that in the wider shape and contour of the unfolding universe there are no accidents. Something is always calling us home.

That was in 2013. But four years later we began looking again for a house in Donegal, this time to purchase. We didn't find one and in 2018 I had a heart attack which seemed to finish off that adventure.

So as I nibbled at the darne of salmon on my breakfast plate in a Donegal hotel in 2019 I began another casual but fateful conversation with the beloved by mentioning the house.

'What about it?' she asked.

'It's up for sale,' I said.

'Is it?' she replied, her face opening in astonishment.

'A holiday home?' I suggested.

'Perish the thought,' she said. 'That's the last thing we need.'

I agreed. 'And we couldn't afford it anyway,' I added.

'But on the other hand,' she said, 'we always need workspaces.'

'We do,' I agreed. 'But could we afford it?'

'We'd need to put everything we have into it,' she said.

'We would,' I agreed.

And we left it at that. And I pondered on the word. Workspace.

A place to work and dream and create new stories and sculptures and find new friends.

For both of us to begin again. To start life all over again. Writing and sculpting. Sculpting and writing. Taking everything from the beginning once more. At our age? It was a ridiculous idea. And completely magical.

We were back in Leitrim that evening before we spoke again about it.

'I suppose an artist's main responsibility is to work,' I mused. 'And a workspace might be very beneficial.'

'Now you're talking,' she said, and she smiled at me like Sarah smiled at Abraham, or like any elderly couple might smile when they stumble on the unchanging wisdom of old age: that heaven in any language is about being, here, now, and that love itself is a kind of empowerment.

There was no other counsellor in the room to advise us against it, on the night we decided to commit ourselves to one more adventure in the hills of Donegal. Apart from MacIntyre's voice in the garden whispering the same old mantra: 'Walk over the cliff, blindfolded.'

We didn't actually speak about the house in Donegal again. We just

knew that it might become the next chapter in our shared adventures.

I made one last visit to Warsaw. I had done so much work there, alone in various apartments writing memoirs, that I felt it would be nice to go back and say farewell. Go back for snow, perhaps. That had worked many times before, winters when the streets were white and my nose red in the freezing fog every time I stuck it outside the door. So back I went again to the streets of Warsaw on the sixth of January, although without much hope of snow in 2020.

I had booked an Airbnb apartment in Praga and on the first morning after my arrival I went to the Orthodox cathedral which was just down the street. They were just finishing the divine service of the nativity for that morning. The porch was wet and people's breath made fog before their faces. Just inside the porch a choir of women were singing in harmony. The crowd was pressing together, squashing each other like ducks trying to cluster around a crust of bread. Suddenly I could see the hierarch coming towards us, a mighty, big man with a dazzling golden cross on his chest. He was handing out holy pictures, images of an icon of the nativity. I was so close I could taste his perfume. I took a holy picture from his hand, pressed my lips to his wrist sleeve in reverence and when I returned to the apartment I put the holy picture on a shelf above the sink.

But I didn't go back again to the church. For the entire month I passed it every day, yet I chose instead to sit in the glass window of Starbucks across the street, or in the eateries of the shopping mall. That was two months before the virus arrived in Ireland. It was scourging the people of Wuhan at that time. But I had no interest in it. What mattered to me was that I felt I had finally drifted past the perimeters of thought. My life seemed like a book that had been written.

My only obsession now was Donegal. With the beloved on FaceTime every evening we discussed how to put money together, what we needed to sell, and what pension savings we could cash in, if we wanted to invest in a workspace and begin life all over again. She drove up to meet the auctioneer and inspect the property. We said we would look again when I returned from Warsaw in February. But we had it sorted. There was no question about pulling out of this one. Unless another heart attack interfered or some global catastrophe was to stymie our plans. Because we wouldn't get another chance to close down life so elegantly and retire to the bliss of life by the ocean. That's how I imagined it. It was an act of love and faith in the absurdity of eternal life. To live as if we had three hundred years more of love to spend.

But to live differently. Let the storyteller be silent. Let the stories and the poetry die. And beyond the words to find a kind of knowing, day by day and moment by moment, in the great belonging of the ocean's music.

It should have been a perfect ending.

What could possibly get in the way?

And this evening, the seventh of June, I am almost finished reading and editing.

It's the last thing I do before sending it to the publisher. And the final few sentences were the last deletion I made from the text:

> *Say after me. I was there. I was present.*
> *I was in my life. I saw my life.*
> *I surfed my life like a wave.*

That's how it ended. But then I felt it was a bit overstated. I was trying to get at the notion that living in the present is like observing yourself, or calling yourself home. It's like being yourself and being aware of yourself at the same moment, so you're following a story all the time. Your own story.

I thought it would be a good template into which I could fit storytelling. But in the end, I felt it was over-egging it. Saying too much. So I left it out. And then.

What?

I was sitting by the window very close to six o clock, when a wind stirred in the trees, tossing them about and making me think of the ocean. It's funny but I hear the ocean in everything now. And the thing about this solitude is that being alone becomes its own company. That's why I was going to put in that sentence. I was going to put it just at the end. But it's better I think to be slightly vague.

And I feel this story is a song, and I am calling myself home. It's a strange feeling and I can't explain it.

Here's another way of putting it: I am my own mother now. I am Buddha watching my own movements, my own tai chi, which I do because my body is stiff from sitting all day in the armchair or at the desk. I have arms as fragile as chicken wings because I have not lived a physically robust life. I develop aches and pains from my elbow to my arse when I sit for too long. I get up and go to the bookshelves, to find someone else's book, because standing at the bookshelves and stretching up to scan the books does my back some good. It relieves the ache in my arse.

One book stands out from the rest. It's odd the way a book can call to me from the shelf sometimes. *Invoking Ireland* by John Moriarty is the book on this occasion. I lift it down and sit with it for a few moments.

It's so eloquent that it makes me wonder why I bother writing anything. Moriarty's work is rich with the passion of the author's extraordinary spirit. He was a man with a big head of shaggy hair, and the eyes of a wise woman. A huge, woolly man, his mind was a cardigan people wanted to hug, and his smile always survived every room he entered. He saw the entire earth and all living things as a vast metaphor for a deeper, invisible knowing.

He was layered like an onion: his ideas needed to be peeled off him. And when someone peeled off one idea, there was another layer of thought inside waiting to emerge, so he often talked himself into a state of exhaustion. He was a whisperer to horses, hares, dogs, dolphins and of course sea birds. Once when he was on an excursion to a small island off the Kerry

> # He was layered like an onion: his ideas needed to be peeled off him.

coast a wind rose as he landed onshore and the day grew so wild that he was forced to take shelter behind a low wall in the ruins of an old church. In the book he says that in the ruined church he was taking shelter from God.

But I don't read his books for philosophical ideas. I read them because they are full of beautiful sentences, crafted poetically. He wrote English as if he were speaking Irish. Even when outlining some philosophical position he could sculpt each thought into a metaphor. For him humanity was not an isolated component that could be measured by scientific examination. He lived his own life as a metaphor, as a surface below which there was great depth.

I see him on the island. In the ancient church. Between the broken walls. Hunkering down. His mop of hair dishevelled. And in the screech of gulls and terns and the wild sea Moriarty can hear a song from deep inside the cosmos. The dolphins and the sea birds sing for him, not just ordinary songs but hymns in praise of all invisible being and all the ground of being. And in these wild songs Moriarty imagines he is experiencing the presence of a God far too terrifying and luminous for his human mind to ever approach. I fidget with the book and flick through a few pages and replace it on the shelf. But this has happened often during the lockdown. Moriarty has entered the room.

When there is nobody in the room the imagination can more easily conjure up a mixed society of ghosts, lovers, old friends and enemies, to entertain, torment, or just lead me forward.

Mary McPartlan was another example, a dear friend I lost during the time of the virus. She didn't die from Covid-19 but from a separate disease on the sixth of April, just before Easter, in a Galway hospital. The day she died I walked to the top of a mountain headland overlooking Drumkeerin, the town where she was born, and I whispered to her, with all the regret that comes after someone has died, 'Mary, I miss you today.'

Later I lit a candle and placed it beside the little golden Buddha statue in my room and then I got on with life. The sun shone all afternoon. But the world was broken and had lost another great storyteller, because singers are the best of storytellers. When we were young she often sat with me when I was alone and I trusted her as a woman whose life was a poem, and whose gifted voice was like balm on any wound. A woman with a smile that opened everyone's heart.

Her smile always implied surprise, always an expression of astonishment on her face. It reflected a kind of awe in her that she was actually alive in the world. On any Leitrim roadside or Galway street she was a walking prayer of gratitude, a hymn in herself not to any particular God, but to the simple mystery of being here.

There were other people who died of everyday causes, but yet the virus ate into the social fabric of their dying. It robbed them of intimacy. It shrouded their funerals in a kind of unease that is alien to such events and robbed families of a normal outpouring of grief.

I remember the first day I started praying. I couldn't tell anyone, but

then there was no one to tell. The only person physically in my life was the beloved and we had put our dreams on hold and quickly found patterns of independence and mutual distancing in order to get on. Boundaries and fences make good lovers. So when we came together in the evening or early morning we relished each other – a touch and kiss as free as young lovers beyond the surveillance of cleric or lawyer.

But prayer is a secret activity. It's a private adventure, a journey to the heart's core. Go inside that room and close the door, they say. Go across that threshold of silence and discover what arises in that interior cosmos.

> *I go to the shed.*
> *It is empty.*
> *I am still.*

I light a candle.
I kneel on the floor.
Being still I can hear my own breathing; I am
*   breathless but my breath quietens; I watch*
*   myself, I am there, here.*
I am watching myself.
And the candle burns.
It is not yet dawn.
It is almost dawn.
I breathe and am glad to be alive. I watch the
*   gladness die. I stand back from it. I rest and*
*   watch myself as if I were a different person.*
I am calling myself home.

And the garden at night had no limits. I could imagine anything. Even such voices whispering in my ear.

I will be a lamp for you. I will show you how to
walk out of the house every day like a shepherd.

Who is he? I wondered. That man with his boat, all those years ago in Donegal. And I can't put a name on him yet, but I will finish the book before six o'clock. And I will go into the house and join the beloved for supper.

And after that I'm not sure.

Usually we watch television. But perhaps not tonight. It's my final night in this severe lockdown. I will come back here. Yes. I want to be alone.

But first I must face the fact that it's time I took down the icons. I cannot avoid it any longer. The icon of the Transfiguration on the wall, the icon of the Resurrection on the shelf, and all the other wooden panels, hand-painted in Belarus, must disappear.

I will pack them in their boxes and wrap them in silk and place them in the press and close them in. I am beyond sheltering in them any longer. This isolation demands I take these little steps into the deep.

And not surprisingly, when it's done, the room looks terribly bare. Only the Buddhas remain: one golden statue, two framed images, a photograph of my teacher and a thangka hanging from the beams.

When I see old film footage of religious processions flanked by police and army colour parties, I wonder did that time really exist. When I see old documentaries about Joe Dolan or long-forgotten showbands crawling around the country in minibuses from one dance hall to another, where thousands of young farmers lined the walls waiting to find the love of their life, squashed against the opposite wall, I wonder did that time really exist. Did we actually live like that, back then? Did those things really matter to us?

But then came a 'time of hope'. Signs that Ireland was emerging from a cultural darkness. The sexual revolution of the Californian beaches arrived in Dublin and a few other urban areas beyond the Pale. If you were in a room with another young person for more than half an hour, and if there was sufficient eye contact to indicate mutual attraction, then a quick bonk was never entirely out of the question.

I missed a lot of that fun. I had been mesmerised by a medieval world of dark cloisters, exotic rituals and men singing melancholic chants about the beauty of crucifixion, while they averted their gaze from denim jeans, cheesecloth blouses and the flesh of young women.

Like many other uncertain boys I was confused by my sexuality, and frightened of the changing world. And in that bliss of sexual illiteracy I was drawn to the safety of an all-male priesthood that played blind man's bluff with philosophy and produced the creator of the cosmos on a silver dish every Sunday morning. We thought that the truth was immutable, that change was illusion. Whereas in fact, change was the only truth.

> Like many other uncertain boys I was confused by my sexuality, and frightened of the changing world.

Now I sit in a room almost in tears because my rich Western world has sunk into a swamp of misfortune, and everything I thought was permanent has been taken away. The world I had held together for a lifetime is being measured by the reaper's blade. The dust of friends is being scattered on the earth without ceremony, and the agony of Calvary haunts every lonely funeral rite. And the possibility that God might indeed have abandoned us wealthy Westerners rises in our minds with the falling away of every new victim. I stay in my room and poke in boxes of old photographs, old memories, talk to old ghosts and finally realise that it is in the fading of photographs and the yellowing of old newspaper cuttings that there exists some truth. This impermanence in everything I touch is the only sustaining thing. No wonder I would turn to prayer.

It's six o'clock. I'm a man of habit. Time for the news on television. Maybe even a boiled egg. I get a text from the beloved, precisely on the hour.

Are you coming in?

She knows just how much I am a creature of habit. She knows how I find comfort in patterns and rituals that follow the clocks and the seasons.

I eat the same porridge every morning at the same time. I take a break at 11 a.m. for coffee. I lunch from one to two and return to work. It's the same in summer. Except I change to muesli. I like to do domestic chores on Thursdays. I like to walk in the markets on Sunday mornings.

But it's in deeper rituals that I find the real anchor of my life.

I have done the pilgrimage to Lough Derg three times. I have walked to the summit of Croagh Patrick. I have even walked around the pilgrim stones in Glencolmcille on the ninth day of June to mark his feast. Just like I mark the feasts of other Christian saints. Just like I mark the Passover, and the beginning of Ramadan. I watch the moons come and go, rise and fall, emerge and wax and wane away.

I take Sunday walks without my phone. I cherish the days of Holy Week in solitude, before the icons of the wounded Christ. I scatter rice in the air and make smoke pujas on Saga Dawa and other Tibetan days of celebration, and I mark the birthday of my teacher and the passing of the Buddha into parinirvana. Not of course forgetting the solstice and cross-quarter days that mark the deep rivets in the cycle of Celtic time: Imbolg or Brigid's Day, the first of May, Bilberry Sunday, Samhain, and the completely transforming light of the mid-winter solstice.

I was born on the feast of the Transfiguration in the Christian calendar, and I once went as far as Belarus just to savour the intensity of devotion that marks that day in an Orthodox monastery.

But I do such things not out of some notion that any or all of those religions have a handle on empirical truth. But because I recognise in all of them a deep and powerful tai chi of the mind, a yearly cycle of mentoring the heart in harmony with the cosmos, the universe, the sky and all that lives and breathes on earth. They are my cog in the cycle of years, the lenses through which I can see what is beautiful in the sky, and on earth and in the hearts of everyone I meet.

For me to live without these punctuation points in the rhythm of all my days and nights, to live without the clock for mealtime, the hour of matins and vespers or midnight prayers for dreamtime, would be to live out of sync with my deepest self. Every Easter is a deeper rebirth, every Christmas a deeper homecoming.

Not that I am a saint or holy person. Not that I observe the rituals of religion with anything more than a soft spiritual self-indulgence, and certainly not that I attend any church. But I am a writer and a storyteller and I cannot aspire to a deft use of metaphor if I do not find some way to live on the inside as well as the outside.

In fact it was on the matter of religion that I first argued with the General.

It was a bleak December day and we were trying to figure out where to put the crib.

Eventually I put it on top of the broken piano, behind the tree, so it's there if people look for it, I said, but it's not in your face.

'I think that's the right balance,' the General agreed.

Then I noticed the cat behind the piano with a bird in her jaws. I released the bird, flung the cat out the door, and inspected the victim. It was a tiny wren, and he had lost a leg and some tail feathers, though he could still fly up against the window, and eventually out into the laurels, when I opened the front door.

'You see,' I said, 'we have saved him. That's what Christmas is all about: kindness.'

'Rubbish,' he declared. 'It has nothing to do with it.'

'Christmas is about the Baby Jesus,' I insisted. 'It's about a mother loving her infant. God loving the world.'

'Sentimental drivel,' he replied. 'It's all poppycock, like stories about fairies and ghosts. It never happened. It was invented by religious zealots and perfected by people who made chocolate boxes in Victorian England.'

'Well, you certainly believe in ghosts,' I said. 'Especially out the Granard road, where you live. Because you told me so.'

A Traveller woman once told the General that on a certain road near Granard there was an old tree, under which she and her husband had camped, and on the following morning a farmer asked them did they sleep well.

'Now that you mention it,' her husband said, 'I was awake all night.'

'Well,' said the farmer, 'don't expect to sleep tonight or any other night if you remain under that tree. Because that is what we call the Hanging Tree.'

'That was only a story,' the General replied. 'You can't believe everything you hear.'

But I didn't let him away with it. I reminded him of the entire account.

'There used to be a shop in Granard,' the Travelling woman had told him, 'that you could be in all night and day, drinking.'

Which her husband was in, late one night, until it was time to go home. And on the way home he passed a big tree, when a man walked out from the shadows, wearing a black coat and a top hat and his face as white as snow, and he walked behind the ass and cart for a mile and a half.'

'Yes, I remember,' the General admitted, 'but it was only a story.'

'And the man went home and told his wife what happened and the next morning her poor husband was lying on the broad of his back in the bed, and his two hands across his chest, and his face as white as the range, and him as dead as a dead fly.'

'Yes,' the General admitted, 'that's how she told it.'

'So you believe in ghosts?'

'We all believe these things,' he roared, 'because and when we want to. They entertain us. Or comfort us. But they're not true. And neither is all that poppycock about Christmas,' he added, with his fist coming down on the piano so ferociously that Baby Jesus went flying across the room.

One morning after I returned from Warsaw at the end of January, I was

standing at the front door of the house in the hills above Lough Allen. Two blackbirds were playing on the lawn for ten minutes, waddling through the leaves, to the right, and then to the left, while the sound of Anna Netrebko wafted from my computer inside the door and blended with the birdsong.

I was waiting for the virus. Each day I did the same.

Until eventually the first cases were announced on the news, and Dr Holohan became our friend in the evenings with his bedside manner, and my days continued, watching blackbirds, and waiting.

The beloved was in good health and we moved around each other by day and night, in various rooms and in the garden. Sometimes she went to her studio for hours and I went to my studio and we would meet in the evenings as if we had come back from distant places.

But her studio and my writing studio were different worlds. Refuges we could vanish into just to find our own quietude. And gradually that spilled out into the common areas. We spent more time in the kitchen together, or more time hoovering and cleaning the floors in the other rooms. But we spent less time communicating. We found a way to be apart even when we were together, so that we didn't risk getting on each other's nerves.

After a week I knew this was the beginning of losing her. Not that she went anywhere. She was still around the house and she was still the same person: wife, artist, mother, mooching about in her studio, digging ridges for potatoes in her garden, coming and going in the car to town when necessary.

The walls are so bare without my icons that I am tempted to get them out again. But I won't. Not yet.

And I can't bear to look at the bookcase. It's like the empty tomb when I look at the shelf where the Christ of Sinai used to stand.

If it weren't for the statue of Buddha sitting on my Samsung woofer, or the figure of Manjushri framed on the wall or the thangka of White Tara hanging from one of the cross beams I'd flee from the room and spend the night watching Netflix.

But not tonight. Tomorrow will be the eighth of June. It ought to have been our day of liberation. I imagined we would be free from lockdown completely by now. We would be travelling up the road tomorrow. We would be in Donegal.

I take a short walk around the outside of the house and through the window I see the beloved in the front room, reading a book. I speak to her through the glass.

'I'll be late tonight. I am still working on the book.'

Then I sit on a bench near the patio, thinking about the great world and all the places I ever visited, and all the storytellers I ever met – some of them writers and singers, some of them possessed by stories and some telling stories to hide the truth. Some conscious of their craft, and others as unaware of their innate skill at telling stories as the blackbird is unaware of the joy he brings to me every evening.

I met a man in China one time who couldn't stop lacerating me with stories. It happened as I was coming out of a tailor's shop in Shanghai one day, after getting stitches in my coat.

The inside lining was in flitters. A thin woman sewed it back together again, with needle and thread. An older woman, who must have been her mother, because she was identical in appearance, boiled soup on a stove behind the counter. Beyond them a door was open and I could see the furniture of a living room, and a picture of Mao Tse-tung on the mantelpiece beneath which were fresh flowers.

I idled on the street outside while she restructured the inside of the coat. Then from the milling crowd of cars, and cyclists, and people on the footpath, a man emerged and reached his hand towards mine.

'You are on Jingling Road,' he said.

I said, 'Yes, I know.'

He said, 'You are a tourist; perhaps you are lost?'

I said, 'I know where I am.'

'And I am Mr Mozart,' he said. 'I am a musician.'

I said, 'I am from Ireland.'

He said, 'Ireland has very nice beer.'

I said, 'Chinese beer is better.'

'Oh yes,' he said, 'Tsingtao is top international beer. I can tell you a story of where I drank my first alcohol.'

We continued like this for some time, and it was clear that he was using me to practise his English.

'Shanghai,' he said, 'is a city influenced by European culture. Charlie Chaplin was a cultural icon. Gene Kelly, also very good. Many stories here of Americans who come to visit us.'

I said, 'My mother was in love with Gene Kelly.'

That shocked him, but I explained that she used to eat chocolates on Sunday afternoons as she sat on the sofa watching old movies. He laughed as if he was deeply familiar with this image.

'Today is the second peak in Chinese civilisation,' he declared. 'The first peak occurred during the Tang dynasty. Now in this time we are witnessing the second peak.'

I said, 'It's also the second trough in Irish history. The first was a famine in the nineteenth century, and now we seem to be entering the second trough.' I elaborated a bit about how hard we had been hit by the financial crisis, but his eyes glazed over.

Later we had bowls of noodle soup in a restaurant with Mrs Mozart, who appeared out of the air and composed texts on her phone with the silent ferocity of an Aran Islander knitting jumpers.

And afterwards we went to People's Park, and sat near Lotus Pond.

Mr Mozart spoke softly. 'I enjoy my whole life,' he declared. 'Things in life are very beautiful, even the lotus. And also I like speaking English, and singing, and playing music and telling stories.'

I said, 'You are truly a man of culture, to sing, play and tell stories.'

'Yes,' he said, deeply appreciative of my comment. 'I have seen *Out of Africa*. I can tell you the entire plot if you have time.'

I didn't.

When I arrived home, a week later, the fields around Mullingar were white with snow. I lit the fires, and sat up until late in the night listening to the flakes whispering on the windowpane. My cat stretched at the fire and I put on my coat and went to the shed for coal, taking a torch with me because there was no moon.

In China Mr Mozart had said, 'Don't take a torch with you if the moon is full. If you take a torch with you, the moon will be broken-hearted.' I think the phrase comes from a love song, and it reflects purity of purpose.

I kept admiring the inside of my coat – the simple thread that perfectly reshaped the pocket, and which was weaved with such pure purpose. I cherished that thread in my coat for a long time afterwards.

The first time I set foot in the townland of Ranafest, a promontory jutting out into the sea and shouldering Carrickfinn, was as a student in the summer college there. I had a soft-spoken bean a' tí with a kind face and an apron like my mother's, who spoke only Irish and the music in her voice carved out a new space in my mind. The adults called her by her first name, and she would give us home-made bread for supper with lashings of rhubarb jam, and sometimes at the table we would dare to say, 'Go raibh maith agat, Kittie.'

There were about seven scholars in her care and we slept in bunks and our bodies ached for the girls down the road in other houses. And when we went to the beach at Carrickfinn, which we called an trá bán, we lusted after the girls as they changed into bathing costumes, and we chased them around the sand dunes when we were all tired of swimming.

But sometimes on that white strand I would slip away

from the other scholars and away from the laughter of girls and I'd stand alone on the rocks wondering about the vast universe and what kind of life might lie ahead for me. I could never quite get the universe into perspective from the window of a suburban childhood bedroom in Cavan. But from the rocks on the edge of the Atlantic I could see clearly.

Even back then my dream was to be a writer, and when my first play was produced at the Peacock Theatre in July of 1987 I wanted to celebrate. So with the beloved we put our bicycles on McGinley's bus in O'Connell Street early one morning and headed to Letterkenny. From there we took another bus going out towards west Donegal, and the driver let us off just beyond Gortahork and we cycled around Bloody Foreland and down through Gweedore and dived into the ocean at Carrickfinn. And we knew we were at home, with each other, in the ocean, on the beach at Carrickfinn.

And even in darker days I often fled to west Donegal for refuge. When I was suffering from depression, and could no longer bear the claustrophobia of Dublin, I fled to the coast. I needed to be alone for a while so I found an old caravan in the sand dunes sitting on cement blocks, with broken windows, and I stayed in it for the entire month of August. Every evening an elderly couple would drive their battered van to the end of the peninsula and I would see them in the distance, standing on the sand dunes silhouetted against the dying sun. They were old but their intimacy against the splendid backdrop of the ocean gave me hope and faith in the possibility of human love. And when autumn came I didn't want to leave, so I rented a chalet on the hill where I could look out at the waves crashing on the sand all day.

Every day that winter I would walk along the strand, thinking about how tectonic plates move around the earth like cracked shell on an egg. I would wonder at the merging of continents, the making of mountains, and the space between ice ages as I gazed out to sea.

There are three rocks off the west Donegal coastline called the Mic O'Gorra (sons of O'Gorra) three pagan swimmers who were turned to stone by Colmcille. Dark as cormorants

> I would wonder at the merging of continents, the making of mountains, and the space between ice ages as I gazed out to sea.

on the distant horizon, I could almost see them come alive on summer mornings, ploughing the waves in search of some pagan refuge beyond the surveillance of the clergy. It gladdened my heart to imagine that any man or woman would risk so much to find their beloved, and depressed me to think that they could be so fossilised in the effort.

But the rocks are still there, the three swimming shadows, and on the beach the white waves still roll along the sand as they have done for millions of years.

The limit of where we could walk in the lockdown was two kilometres

but that was sufficient for me to get to the top of the mountain, near Spion Kop, along the Miners' Way. Almost every second day I took the Miners' Way across the hills, a meandering path that the miners used long ago when they were coming and going from work in pits at the top of the mountain.

A retired miner was telling me one time that they had home-made lanterns for going over the hills to the mines on winter nights. A candle was stuck into a half potato and the potato placed at the bottom of a jam jar. Then a lid with perforated holes was twisted tight and so each miner could walk in the wind with his lantern lighting the way. And as well as lanterns the miners attached bells to wooden posts along the route so that when the pathways were covered with snow they could hear the bells and knew in which direction to walk.

On the evening of the seventh of June I took to the path again, and before the sun had fallen into the horizon I was sitting at the top, sitting still and gazing in the direction of Croagh Patrick, and trying to squeeze myself into the present moment, like a frog in the grass.

It's not that I want to be a frog. Life can be dangerous enough, without lawnmowers to the left and the cat's paw to the right, but frogs always remind me of old Zen masters.

So I walked the mountain with Zen masters that had frogs' faces, longing for the hills of Donegal which I had no access to on account of the lockdown, and when I came down from the mountain I was ready to sleep.

But I didn't. I went back to the studio and played back programmes from Raidio na Gaeltachta on the soundbar. At least the sweet voice of a Donegal presenter could be a consolation for not actually being there. Not that I understand Donegal Irish, but in the native Irish vowels I can hear the waves falling on the strand at Carrickfinn. I kept the volume low so that the presenter's presence remained at a distance, but still as soothing as the bean a' tí in my far-away childhood.

I dozed and slept, and when I woke it was dark, and Thich Nhat Hanh was speaking.

'You are only one step away from happiness,' I could hear him say. 'Bliss is like a flower; just reach out and touch it.'

There has been a full moon

these past few nights – strong and bright and high enough to flood the bedroom with a pallid hue.

I tossed and turned in bed. I couldn't sleep. So today, while I was mowing the grass, I promised myself some special time alone.

And since today I finish the book, and tomorrow is – or was – supposed to be our liberation day from the lockdown and the day afterwards is the feast of Colmcille, my pagan Celtic Christian mentor-deity, I feel it would be auspicious to keep vigil this night until dawn. To lean again on the calendar of saints, the cycles of the moon. To punctuate again the present moment with icons of eternity. To pause and hope and pray.

The moon is still full. The garden is as clear as coral under water. Something out there beckons me. And staying awake might make more sense than just tossing and turning in the bed for hours.

So now I go to the woodpile and gather in silence, without any sound apart from the owl in the spruce tree, hooting in the key of D. I get more briquettes for the stove. Even in June a fire is required in my little studio shed at night.

All over Ireland it is evening time. The wheel turns. In another few hours silence will fall with the moonlight, along the empty streets, and in the graveyards, and on the ocean beaches, and across the bogs and in the housing estates, and in the city centres and here around me in the hills above Lough Allen. Silence will come like an invisible virus on all the trees in the garden.

But I will not sleep.

How could it be possible that everything would change in such a brief moment in that far-away wet market in the city of Wuhan? And how could it happen that a simple virus, a tiny bug, would find its way through airports and onto planes, and from one continent to another, glued to the lungs of innocent carriers, until it was everywhere and the economy of the world was on the verge of collapse?

Everybody wondered was it a deadly enemy, or just the slightest modification of the cosmic order that might make humans more fully conscious of the mystery and presence of being here.

I wondered about that too.

I prayed Christian prayers to be delivered from the plague. I prayed Buddhist prayers to remain in equanimity if I was struck down. I even started reading Jung, and listening to books by analysts on the internet, to see if I could do a speed course in all that modern mysticism of twentieth-century psychoanalysis and make sense of my life, or the world that is around me.

But mostly I was defeated by those endeavours and ended up with a glass of wine watching Netflix. And then the morning would come. And another beautiful day, where all the birds and wild animals in the garden seemed more lively than usual and I suspected even as early as the end of March that the lack of pollution, the lack of planes overhead, and the lack of diesel rising from the roads had cleaned up the world so much that already the animals moved about with a new confidence in their stride.

At least the pheasant strutted around the pond with great confidence, picking up buckwheat that the beloved had put out for smaller birds. And in the sky one hundred geese flew towards the north-west, probably coming from Wexford I guessed, en route to Canada. They would stop in Sligo near where Dermot Healy used to live. I watched the V move near the clouds and thought of Dermot – or maybe imagined I saw him there, in a different form, still wild and free and leading the way.

Sometimes I'd see my beloved pass through the room, holding a bunch of flowers in one hand and a knife in the other, as she searched for a vase. Respecting her silence, her privacy, her own mystical journey into whatever labyrinth of sorrow or joy was enveloping her.

Her presence out there in the house, beyond this room, makes all this room seem silly. Even the candlesticks and bells, the incense holders and all the other trinkets of religiosity are childish games compared to the wonder of being with another human being. And yet all day she is out there in her studio and I'm in here in mine.

Isolated even from each other. Why is that, I wonder?

I remember looking out the window of a hotel in Shanghai at seven o'clock one Monday morning in 2011. I was on the twenty-first floor and the Irish minister for finance was on the television, telling the world that Ireland was broke. Opposite me another hotel, like a cliff of glass, reached forty

To look at Shanghai from a skyscraper is like seeing an ocean for the first time and trying to imagine all the possibilities of hope
in that deep.

storeys into the sky, and I could see into rooms where the curtains were open and people were coming from their morning showers and staring blankly out windows.

I saw a naked man at one window, and beside him another man in a dressing robe. They were gazing at the smoggy city below us, the tiny cars on the highways, and the sprawling ocean of humanity that is Shanghai.

Then the naked man sat down and the other guy rested his

hand on the naked fellow's shoulder, as if to comfort him. Perhaps they too were watching the Irish minister for finance on CNN.

To look at Shanghai from a skyscraper is like seeing an ocean for the first time and trying to imagine all the possibilities of hope in that deep. Because China is an ocean of humanity, and what could be better than that?

And being one among so many in that wall of glass gave me a sense of belonging, similar to what gannets probably feel on Skellig Michael.

I headed into town to meet a friend, past neon screens dancing with Chinese characters. Though I might as well have been looking at cobwebs, because I can't read Chinese.

Everywhere there were bicycles and scooters, giggling girls, and old men on street corners selling watches and handbags.

Near Jing'an Park a man was crawling along the pavement. He had a single deformed leg and he dragged it behind him like the tail of a fish. Like a swimmer doing butterfly strokes, he flung his torso forward, all the while pushing his begging bowl ahead of him, and trying to get into the centre of the pavement so that it would be difficult for people to ignore him.

On Nanjing Road two prostitutes spoke to me. A middle-aged woman and a bubbling teenager, with purple lips, and black hair in a bun. Clearly they thought I was a pure eejit if they expected me to go down a dark alley with them just because they admired my hair, pulled my beard and remarked on how enormous my feet were.

'Everything about you is so big,' one said, with a kind of

cartoon innocence that she had probably picked up from movies about girls who work the streets. I told her I was from a place called Leitrim and that there were no flies on us, apart from dead ones. I told her I was born in Cavan, where we ate our dinner out of a drawer, and closed it if anyone came to the door.

'We're not fools,' says I defiantly. 'Ireland may be broke but the country people will survive. So no, I'm not going down the alleyway with either you or your mammy, but thank you for the compliment about my feet.'

And off I went, although I'm not convinced that they fully understood me. And no matter where I travelled, whether to London, Shanghai or New York, I always wanted home. And no matter how many stories I could remember from the seven corners of the world about how it was before the virus, I always ended up with memories of the ocean and the beach in Donegal bubbling up in the moonlight as I sat by the stove.

On the streets of Mullingar I was a hunter. On the streets of Shanghai I was hunted. Sometimes by young female sex workers at the doors of bars, who saw me from far off and pursued me initially with the question, 'Are you American?'

I felt so relieved when they went away that I fled into a temple for refuge.

I lit incense sticks and went up to the shrine room and had a moment of time-out, kneeling on a cushion while people around me did prostrations. One old man looked like Mao Tse-tung, and it crossed my mind that there is at least one thing to be grateful for in this life, and that is that Mao never became Taoiseach of Ireland.

In Jing'an Park an old man with grey hair and a beard sat on the pavement and played a small two-stringed instrument, with a bow. White chalk dust covered the instrument like snow.

On Yan'an Road a white wedding limo was changing lanes when it bashed into the side of a Volkswagen Bora. The Volkswagen ended up in the flowerbeds, its side ripped asunder and a clump of potted plants on the bonnet. The bride and her party got out and sauntered over to the park, smoking and laughing and taking photographs. Police arrived and made sketches of the scene and argued with the two drivers.

Finally, on Jingling, a street of musical instruments, and old rusting bicycles that must have been around since before the time of Mao, I found my friend.

She gave me a painting of a plum tree, blossoming in winter, which signifies strength and fortitude.

Then I walked back to my hotel, through the streets where women with masks swept the leaves and old men pushed carts laden down with oranges, and a woman in a scarf beat the dust out of a carpet that hung between a lamppost and a traffic light. I wanted to ask them all did they know how distressed poor old Ireland was, or did they even know we existed. But some of them might not even have a television set, I thought.

And when the virus first appeared in Wuhan and I saw women walking the streets wearing masks, I was reminded again of that time. But in June Wuhan appeared to have beaten the virus. And now we were in lockdown. And I was watching Wuhan celebrating, the entire city lit up like a gaudy neon carousel, while outside my door the only sound was that of hungry cattle, lost lambs, hooting owls and a vixen fox tearing the night asunder with her cries.

It was well after midnight.

The magpies had long ago settled down for the night but there was one of them cackling like an agitated mother bird. I could hear her through the window and realised it was she who had wakened me.

It was unusual to hear a magpie cackling outside the window at one o'clock in the morning, but perhaps she had a difficult baby up there in the spruce tree. It can't be easy for mother birds, I thought, minding little ones at night.

Years ago I had birds in the attic of Shandonagh House near Mullingar. I would lie listening to them for weeks, shrill and squawky, and I imagined their blind beaks emerging from broken shells.

But they had been well minded in that attic, I thought, because after a few days the scalding voices grew deeper and more mellow.

That was the year the Queen of England came to Ireland.

Another heroic mother who didn't have much comfort either, as she walked up an endless amount of stairs, without a crutch, while the cameras of the world crawled all over her face.

When she held the spade in the Phoenix Park and shovelled clay onto a new tree, for the benefit of more cameras, I felt sympathy for her, and for her lady of the bedchamber, who was wearing a blue dress and who held the queen's handbag as the queen held the spade.

Not that holding a handbag is hard work, but the lady of the bedchamber has many other duties to the queen and I took a great interest in her because she once lived a mile away from me in Cavan, in the grand estate of Farnham, where her husband, a tall, upright and handsome figure, was lord until his death in 2001.

I met her once when a school companion and I cycled our bicycles as far as the gates of the estate and braved it up the long pebbled avenue on foot, into the splendid lawns, just as Lady Farnham was getting into her station wagon.

I had often been to the orchards on the estate, to get apples and plums, but I had never been in this forbidden space of sequoia and cedar tree, of flat lawn and magnolia petal on her private grounds. My companion and I trembled in her presence and her posh accent terrorised us.

'Can I help you?' she said, stroking her long sandy hair away from her eyes, and showing her face to be sharp and beautiful. We fumbled for words.

'Would you like to sponsor a line for Concern?' we asked in flat Cavan accents. It must have sounded like gobbledegook to her, but after a brief interrogation she finally extracted from us that we were collecting money for a charity walk. She said she'd be delighted to give us a donation and she even offered us a lift back into town, four miles away.

Our bicycles were in the ditch at the front gate, but neither of us could resist such intimacy, so we hopped into her station wagon and went back to Cavan like men who had found the Golden Fleece, or negotiated the security of earth with an alien from another planet. In leather upholstery we giggled as we floated past the rhododendron where our bicycles lay hidden, for we could easily collect them on the morrow. There was always time for everything in those days, and we lived our youth leisurely as if we had oodles of the stuff.

Little did we realise that in fact my friend had very little time left, because a few years later he was swept to his death in the sea off Donegal. A companion with him saw him in the water and shouted at him to hold on, that he would get a rope. But the salty waves took the drowning boy away and his body was never found.

The Queen of England is still strong and still walks without a crutch and perhaps sometimes she listens to birds in the palace attic, or perhaps her lady of the bedchamber occasionally recalls the glory of the dawn chorus along the shoreline of a Cavan lake. And perhaps my school friend heard some benign presence singing to him in the merciless waves of the Atlantic. I suppose it's not for us to say.

On one occasion I thought I saw my mother on the street going into Tesco, but it was only a ghost, a tiny bit of shrapnel glistening in a remote region of my unconscious mind. When things were relaxed in early May I saw two old men sitting on separate benches near the river and I thought I was walking into a Beckett play.

The first man was tall and very heavy, and he was lugging his hip along with difficulty, and sat down exhausted on the nearest bench. The second man arrived a few moments later, as small and wiry as a jockey, with a baseball cap sheltering

'Grief is like an amputation,' they agreed. 'It can't be named nor shared. It gets stuck inside the body, like a stone in the chest.'

his eyes. He sat on a second bench at the appropriate social distance.

'I hear you can get the virus on public benches,' the first man joked. He spoke towards the river.

Then the man on the other bench said, 'They have it in Cavan, but they'll give it to no one.' He too spoke to the river.

Like characters in a Beckett play they were bleak. They didn't laugh. Their jokes were not funny. And each contribution was followed by silence. It wasn't what they said that absorbed me. It was the silences between each comment.

'I lost my wife a month ago,' the big man said. 'She died before the virus. I'm glad she's not here to see all this.'

It turned out that the second fellow had been widowed too, just before Christmas, and that changed everything. The strangers continued in single disjointed phrases, to share the pain of losing their loved ones.

'I feel I have to keep the house tidy,' the little jockey confessed. 'Because she used to keep it so clean and neat.'

Fragmented sentences rose from silence and into the wind, and then fell back again into the silence.

'Grief is like an amputation,' they agreed. 'It can't be named nor shared. It gets stuck inside the body, like a stone in the chest.'

I tried to hear the river. I tried to listen for some car in the distance heading for Dublin. But I could only hear the wind, and the muffled and strangled grief that was embodied in their speechlessness.

So I spent the night keeping vigil with all the dead I could remember,

who had been lost in the stench of Covid-19, or down all the years of my life. Such voices rise easily in dreams and in the darkness before dawn.

I swam out past anxieties about health, worries about money, and the paranoia that attends all our well-laid plans for the future. I swam to find some comforting stranger voice, some bodhisattva song or some hymn from the monasteries of the Egyptian desert. But in the half-awake dreams of midnight it's difficult to distinguish between angelic choirs and the cackling of restless magpies.

'Do you hear him?'
'Yes.'
'Who?'

'Somebody lamping. Night fishing. Under the shadow of the mountain.'

'What do you hear?'

'Clear water of the estuary, rising in a bucket.'

'What do you see?'

'Burning rushes.'

'What do you know?'

'I know he gathers. Cooks fish.'

'But will we meet him?'

'I don't know. The sun will rise. Perhaps he will vanish like smoke. And the fields shall be empty again. But in a new way.'

It is dawn. I stand in the garden as the shadows melt. The lake is sleeping. The mountain beyond is silent in the half light. I can't see it clearly yet.

The wind blows the trees and an alder branch falls against a cherry tree and begins creaking. The wood of two trees meets and joins in the wind, adding to my desolation. Because I am desolate now.

The long-eared owl disturbs me too; he came to the high spruce tree where the magpies had abandoned their nest. I heard him in April one night when I went to the shed to get more briquettes. The soft hoot, round as a ball of wool beating out each night for three nights. Then he went. Either he got a mate or moved on somewhere else, I thought.

But now he's back. He's like a messenger of death and it unnerves me.

'Do you see the mountain?' a voice whispered when I was sleeping.

'Yes.'

'What colour is it?'

'Brown. Purple and brown.'

'Now listen.'

'Yes.'

'What do you hear?'

'A boat on the estuary.'

'Be precise.'

'The oar slushing in and out of the tide. The creaking of the oar on the oar locks. Wood on wood.'

'Now look again at the mountain. What do you see?'

'Errigal: blue and grey.'

'Is there a connection?'

'Yes. The sound of the oar is turning the mountain blue.'

'He will try again tomorrow night. To burn rushes. To light his fire. Slop his bucket of water. He will gather the smoke from his fire and try to prevent it dissolving into the sky. He will turn the mountain blue with the sound of his oars. He will turn his head and look at the clouds. All the time he is hoping we will find him. So that he too can exist for a while. And in the meantime, in this never-ending time, we will never find him. But we will keep searching.'

I kept wondering what would become of us. How would we be transformed by this thing in the air?

I was lighting candles in the evenings, and I remained alone in my room for hours.

'Go to your room,' the desert monks used to say, 'and your

room will teach you everything.'

So I did. But that was at the beginning. That's when I made religious shrines in every corner, focal points that opened like a portal into the soul of the world. I lit a candle and the icons glowed behind it, and I watched the flame flicker on the faces of every Buddha and all the Christian saints.

It was as if everyone in heaven had come together: Jesus, Mary, Buddha, Shiva, Moses and all the prophets of Islam. They were all working together to comfort me.

And it didn't seem to matter if my icons were Christian or Buddhist or just family photographs, they were all vectors of hope and love in a dark time. But now the room is empty. And I walk in the garden. Because I can't just remain in the dark, with my hopes like a blanket around me. Time comes, dawn comes, and I need to step out.

Whenever I lit a candle during the lockdown I imagined someone else was doing the same thing at the same moment. It was as if I was standing before a single flame with strangers at my side, sharing the same gentle light in the dark. And there was no need to call it prayer; it was a human gesture, an act of faith, without any particular object.

When I stood at the window during the daylight hours I saw and I heard the world outside – the beautiful blackbird and magpie and all the little finches on the branch of a tree. One day I even saw a fox, exhausted, crossing the lawn.

But when I lit a candle at twilight I saw and I heard the world inside. And then I knew I was not alone.

Then waking felt like dreaming. And sleeping felt like waking up.

'You like birds?' she asked.
'Dreams,' I replied.
'You like dreams?' she asked.
'Birds,' I replied.
'Which birds?' she wondered.
'Black,' I said.
'Some birds are not black.'
'Mine are,' I said.
'You're dreaming,' she said. 'You need to wake up.'

A New Day

The first birds have begun to sing, welcoming in this eighth day of June. The eve

of a feast day. The sun is already above Sliabh an Iarainn. The woodland is glistening green, flowing and billowing in the morning breeze and it is full of music.

So it's not just grief that has been amplified – the virus has made everything else more intense as well. Colours are deeper. Sounds are bigger. And even silence is not an emptiness anymore. That is where I feel the deepest change has come. No matter what is ahead for me or for any of us, be it economic hardship or physical struggles or ultimately death itself.

Did we really forget that single truth on which all hope is based? That death is everyone's companion, already here, inside, or in the corner of the room, waiting for our time? And have we noticed him again? And is that what makes the silence deeper?

Not an emptiness anymore. But a space we begin to touch

anew and wherein we find defiant hope. Certainly the silence in the garden feels quieter and richer.

The world was never this quiet in my entire life. Not even when I was a child on Christmas morning walking in the snow around the golf links on the edge of Cavan town. Not even in Mongolia crossing the empty land in a jeep full of holy monks who didn't do much talking from one day to the next.

It was never this quiet even in the empty churches and cloisters of my youth where I first learned to pray.

In Maynooth in the early seventies hundreds of clerical students would cram into the main chapel every Sunday morning to sing their hearts out. But on Holy Week they went silent. Everyone went on retreat. Everyone went into a time of isolation and reflection. The cut-stone arches and vaults and corridors fell silent. The retreat master explained that on Good Friday the Christian world held its breath – Christ was dead, really dead, he said, lost in the oblivion of a burial shroud.

'So we keep vigil from Good Friday evening until Easter morning,' he said, 'contemplating that dead thing, and that dead time and that dead space.'

Back then we believed in a realm of non-existence which was made visible in the liturgies of the church – a dimension beyond space and time, that mattered for us. A ground of being that held the universe, like a mother might hold a newborn infant.

But in the dead space between Good Friday and Easter Sunday that dimension went dark. God was offline. No word escaped the silence that fell on the cloisters and the corridors and the refectory with devastating elegance.

Those retreats opened silences inside my own psyche and allowed me for the first time to access the underbelly of my own murky unconscious mind.

Not that I would have used terms like 'unconscious' or 'mindfulness' back then to describe what for me was just prayer. But back then things were different.

The virus sometimes felt like a darkness. And yet the garden where I passed the time in the hills above Lough Allen was never as beautiful, or never as peaceful as it appears today at dawn. Even while grief still seeps up out of the ground, it is beautiful. This garden where I stand now in these hills above Lough Allen was never as beautiful, or never as peaceful as it is today in this moment.

I am always astonished by small things in this space: the budding trees, the goofy gait of a pheasant, or two crows on an oak branch wobbling in the wind as they sing their lamentations in the evening, like cowled monks, or like old, bewildered men.

But this morning is special. Because I chose today. The spring air is cleaner than it used to be. Birds sing with a deeper resonance. The apple trees shed their petals and fatten their fruit with an astonishing defiance. As if nature itself carried a coded message: everything will be OK in the end. Hope may seem lost with each new death but love has become more visible in every hospital corridor in the world.

'Let's begin again.'

That's how I put it. That's what I said to the beloved at the start of the lockdown.

'Let's begin a new life, as if we were young. Let's drive around the world in a camper van. Let's find a place to live beside the ocean. Let's roll in the waves, rejoice in the sea, and make love until dawn in the back of a van.'

Love didn't seem possible or easy on the twelfth of March at our age. But now, after twelve weeks of isolation and lockdown, trying to shepherd each other through the wasteland of fear, love seemed not just possible, but absolutely necessary.

I know it's too early for her to be up yet, but soon the beloved too will wake and dress and move to the kitchen to make coffee and she will wonder where I am. Not that she would worry. She knows the studio is my shelter, and that no clock can completely curtail a writer's unruly imagination.

But nonetheless I will go when the time is right to the kitchen window, and tap it if she is there, and I will remind her of everything.

Shaping three vowels with my lips. 'Donegal.'

And she will give me a thumbs-up. Because that is our code. My libido might be weak but the spirit is strong, and the will, to begin again. We can never lose hope. We will dance somewhere yet.

I've always loved dancing. And she loves the music. And we are never too old for dancing.

The house in Donegal is waiting for us and was always waiting for us.

It's been waiting all through the lockdown because when we finally bought it on the twenty-fifth of March, it was too late and we couldn't visit it.

It sat there for decades, waiting for me as I wandered around Shanghai, New York, London, Paris, Ulaanbaatar or Warsaw. It sat there under Errigal, waiting for me to complete my journey and close my narrative and turn the key in the door and open into its strangeness, and begin something different. No matter where I wandered. In cities far away. The universe was not indifferent. There was a shape unfolding in the itch and bounce of every tiny molecule of space that would prescribe for me the path to that door.

I chose the eighth of June because I thought the lockdown would surely be over by then, by now, and I would be in Donegal today. But I am not. I must wait longer. I must hope and believe that my little dreams will come true, but I have no certainty. None of us have.

Maybe some accident at the last moment will trigger a disaster and I still won't ever see those things I have been dreaming of at the seashore. Or perhaps it is only in my heart that they will happen, as dreams of the future. Because the virus makes everything uncertain, and even what futures we would have once presumed, we can no longer presume.

And even now, as the lockdown melts and dissolves gradually through the coming weeks, it's only reasonable to conclude that we don't know the half of what might be up ahead – from this virus or from further mutations, with or without a vaccine, or in a world where the global economy may be faltering in ways it has never done before in history. So who would guess tomorrow in those circumstances? Or who would presume the future?

All I can say is that even I have finally accepted that God is offline indefinitely. All channels of communication are closed. Until further notice.

We only have poetry now, and each other.

'But sir,' she said, 'a tornado is coming.'
'More wine, then,' I said, 'and we will teach this storm a thing or two about lovemaking.'

The bees are awake, already busy. Perhaps I should speak to them. Tell them that I cannot explain how I ended up in Donegal on the edge of the ocean. I could assure them that there was no intention, no plan, no wisdom attached to the move. It was just an accident, accumulating through time like a tree that grows or a tree that falls. Because it's where the

WHAT IS BEAUTIFUL IN THE SKY

book ends. Where the story ends. Where the storyteller surrenders to silence, and to the calm and quiet sea.

And even if it doesn't happen, I will have written that it happened. I will have spoken my faith. Even if I have to wait until July, perhaps another month or two. A few years maybe. Or even if I never actually break out of this isolation. Even if I never actually get there.

It will be the way the story ended.

So I told it to the bees, and they heard me. It was my faith, spoken in words, sculpted in time, through the telling of it.

I know they heard me because even as this grief still seeps up out of the ground, the bees have begun again – to gather and hum, to turn the mountain blue. And I can hear them singing and I tell it to them again, that this garden where we stand now in these hills above Lough Allen was never as beautiful, or never as peaceful, as it is now, in this moment.

Acknowledgements

My thanks to my agent, MGOC, and to the staff at Hachette for all their wonderful work in making this book possible.

And my very special thanks to Ciara Doorley, my editor at Hachette, for her wonderful work in helping me shape and imagine this book.

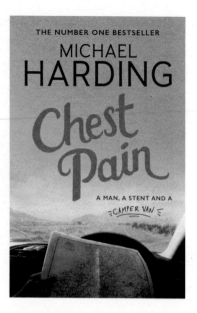

In late 2018, Michael Harding was in a hotel room in Blanchardstown experiencing severe pains in his chest. He eventually phoned an ambulance and was admitted to hospital, suffering from an acute heart attack. Here, in *Chest Pain*, he looks at the months before the heart attack when he kept the signs of failing health from his beloved and instead retreated into solitude – and with his own inimitable style and humour takes us with him through the months after a stent had been inserted in his heart, where he travels the roads of Donegal in a camper van in a journey back to the beloved, and to himself.

Chest Pain is a thought-provoking, spell-binding memoir about togetherness and what it means to be alive.

Also available as an ebook

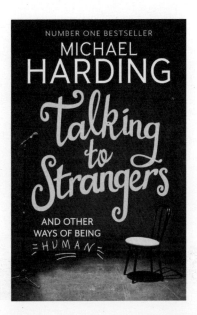

Too much wine and a casual browse of an airline website – this is how Michael Harding found himself in a strange flat in Bucharest in early January, which set the tone for the rest of that year.

After an intense stint in a high-profile production of *The Field*, Harding returned to the tranquil hills above Lough Allen and started to plan some dramatic changes to his little cottage. Surely an extension would give him a renewed sense of purpose in life as he approached old age.

But as the walls of his home crumbled, so too did his mental health, and he fell, once again, into depression – that great darkness where life feels like nothing more than a waste of time.

And yet, it is in that great darkness that we discover what really makes us human.

Talking to Strangers is a book about love, about the stories we share with others, and the stories we leave behind us.

Also available as an ebook

'In public or on stage, it's different. I'm fine. I have no bother talking to three hundred people, and sharing my feelings. But when I'm in a room on a one-to-one basis, I get lost. I can never find the right word. Except for that phrase – hold me.'

Michael Harding's wife has departed for a six-week trip, and he has been left alone in their home in Leitrim. Faced with the realities of caring for himself for the first time since his illness two years before, Harding endeavours to tame the 'elephant' – an Asian metaphor for the unruly mind. As he does, he finds himself finally coming to terms with the death of his mother – a loss that has changed him more than he knows.

Funny, searingly honest and profound, *Hanging with the Elephant* pulls back the curtain and reveals what it is really like to be alive.

Also available as an ebook

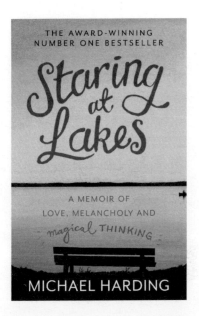

THE AWARD-WINNING
NUMBER ONE BESTSELLER

Staring at Lakes

A MEMOIR OF
LOVE, MELANCHOLY AND
magical THINKING

MICHAEL HARDING

* Bord Gáis Energy Book of the Year 2013 *

Throughout his life, Michael Harding has lived with a sense of emptiness – through faith, marriage, fatherhood and his career as a writer, a pervading sense of darkness and unease remained.

When he was fifty-eight, he became physically ill and found himself in the grip of a deep melancholy. Here, in this beautifully written memoir, he talks with openness and honesty about his journey: leaving the priesthood when he was in his thirties, settling in Leitrim with his artist wife, the depression that eventually overwhelmed him, and how, ultimately, he found a way out of the dark, by accepting the fragility of love and the importance of now.

Staring at Lakes started out as a book about depression. And then became a story about growing old, the essence of love and marriage – and sitting in cars, staring at lakes.

Also available as an ebook and audio book

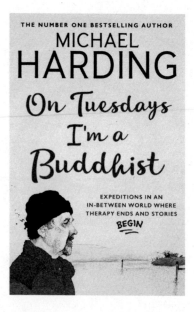

THE NUMBER ONE BESTSELLING AUTHOR
MICHAEL
HARDING
On Tuesdays
I'm a
Buddhist

EXPEDITIONS IN AN
IN-BETWEEN WORLD WHERE
THERAPY ENDS AND STORIES
BEGIN

One day in the summer of 2016, Michael Harding's wife brought an unusual gift home from Warsaw. All of a sudden, he found himself falling back into the old religious devotions of an earlier time. The meaning he had found through years of engagement with therapy began to dissolve.

Here, Harding examines the search for meaning in life which keeps him fastened to the idea of god.

After many therapy sessions focused on an effort to uncover personal truth, and long solitary months on the road with a one man show, Harding is finally led to an artists' retreat in the shadow of Skellig Michael.

Mixing stories from the road with dispatches from his Irish Times columns, On Tuesdays I'm a Buddhist is a spell-binding and powerful book about the human condition, the narratives we weave around the self, and the ultimate bliss of living in the present moment.

Also available as an ebook